MARCHING ON TOGETHER

MARCHING ON TOGETHER

Tales from Elland Road

Volume One
Edited by Rick Broadbent

TALES FROM
www.talesfrom.com

First published in Great Britain in 2018
by Tales From

Printed and bound by Page Bros Ltd

Jacket design and photography by www.stonecreativedesign.com

Scarf featured on jacket supplied by www.savile-rogue.com

ISBN 978-1-912249-04-6

Tales From Ltd
107 Jupiter Drive, Hemel Hempstead, Herts HP2 5NU
Registered company number: 9082738
www.talesfrom.com
info@talesfrom.com

MARCHING ON TOGETHER

CONTENTS

THE EDITOR – RICK BROADBENT

Rick's first football game was half-decent. It was the European Cup semi-final against Barcelona, and Leeds won 2-1. Not that he was bothered, having been dragged there by his dad who reasoned this was a landmark event that no Leeds-born six-year-old should miss. A season ticket-holder during the original decline, he has worked at *The Times* since the days when there was a Yorkshire patch, now covering a range of sports, writing books, trying to get kids into reading and writing via www. presspackers.com, but mostly wishing he had appreciated that it was not the norm for Leeds to spend Wednesday nights turning over Johan Cruyff in front of more than 50,000 people. On Twitter he is @ricktimes.

THE WRITERS

ROB BAGCHI

Born in Wakefield the day before a 2-0 victory over Southampton, Rob lived there for the first 18 years of his life. He worked for Sportspages book shops in London and Manchester for ten years, joined the sports desk of the *Guardian* in 2002 and left for the *Telegraph* in 2013, where he remains. He co-wrote *The Unforgiven* which was first published in 2002 and has subsequently been reprinted in yellow, green and, finally, white covers, as well as three other books. Rob lives in London – the main reason he gave up his season ticket ten years ago; the others being two young children and exasperation after a spiky phone call with Ken Bates.

DANIEL CHAPMAN

Born and raised in Leeds, but refined a nerdish fervour for Leeds United during his enforced exile, and returned to the city and a season ticket as soon as he could. He has co-edited Leeds United fanzine *The Square Ball* since 2011, taking it through its 25th anniversary, and seven nominations for the Football Supporters' Federation Fanzine of the Year award, winning twice. He has written a film and a book about Howard Wilkinson's title-winning team at Leeds, both called *Do You Want to Win?*, and a new history of the club called *100 Years of Leeds United* to be published in 2019. On Twitter he is @MoscowhiteTSB.

ANTHONY CLAVANE

Also born and brought up in Leeds, Anthony is the author of *Promised Land*, a social and cultural history of Leeds United, which was named Sports Book of the Year in 2010. His second book, *Does Your Rabbi Know You're Here?*, was nominated for Football Book of the Year. His latest book, *A Yorkshire Tragedy*, looks at how the county's sporting landscape has changed since the 1980s. He has had three plays performed in Leeds by Red Ladder. *Playing the Joker*, about rugby league and Yorkshire identity, which was originally at the West Yorkshire Playhouse and is now touring Yorkshire; *Promised Land* and *Leeds Lads* were both put on at Leeds Carriageworks and co-written with Nick Stimson.

A journalist for 28 years Anthony now writes a weekly arts column for the *Yorkshire Post*. For many years he covered sport for the *Sunday Mirror*. He also writes for the *New European*, the *Blizzard*, the *Guardian* and the *New Statesman*.

ROBERT ENDEACOTT

Robert Endeacott is a life-long Leeds fan, born in the LGI and brought up in Beeston LS11 where he still lives. Writer of books, often about Leeds, and screenplays, published works include *One Northern Soul* followed by *No More Heroes*, as well as the factual Leeds supporter book *Fanthology*, with Graeme Garvey. The ironically titled bestselling novel *Dirty Leeds* arrived in 2009, and the sequel, *Disrepute – Revie's England*, followed. Due to publisher closure, then came *After Extra Time (Dirty Leeds Uncut)*, which is the extended version of *Dirty Leeds*. Other books include the unauthorised biography of The Stranglers, *Peaches – a Chronicle of The Stranglers, 1974–1990*, and the factual book about the Zulu Warriors gang of 1980s Birmingham, *Hunting the Hooligans*, co-written with the former chief officer of the police's Operation Red Card, Mike Layton. In 2018 comes

Robert's eagerly awaited novel about John Charles' departure from Leeds to Juventus in 1957.

PHIL HAY

Born in Penicuik, near Edinburgh, in 1980 and a Heart of Midlothian supporter from the day when football first registered. University brought Phil south of the border at the age of 17 and he has worked as a journalist for the past 18 years, 15 of those on the *Yorkshire Evening Post*. As the paper's chief football writer he has covered Leeds United home and away since 2006 and followed the many dramas at Elland Road. A dad of two patient girls, neither of whom look like catching the bug.

ADAM POPE

Born in Liverpool and raised on the Wirral, he watched both Everton and Liverpool as a kid in the 1970s and early 1980s, before opting for the Blues. Adam finally moved to Yorkshire as a teenager to study at Huddersfield Polytechnic. Mixing with supporters of clubs outside the top flight he soon learnt that 'administration' and 'relegation' were common parlance as well as 'title-winning' and 'balmy European nights'.

This clearly held him in good stead to cover Leeds United, which he began doing for the BBC in 2005 after careers in builders' merchants and brewing. Elland Road prior to that had been a place of intimidating misery, as Everton had almost always lost there during his lifetime. That he now is based high up in the West Stand, on the gantry with headphones and a microphone, commentating on one of the most fascinating and unique clubs, is still beyond his comprehension at times. To do so alongside Noel Whelan makes him realise just how much Leeds United means to so many people within the city and beyond.

JAMES RIACH

His first match report was published in *Leeds Leeds Leeds* magazine in 2009 and since then he was worked as a journalist for Sky Sports, the Press Association and the *Guardian*. James spent five years at the *Guardian*, where he wrote extensively about the ownership of Leeds United under Massimo Cellino, GFH Capital and Ken Bates, when there was rarely a slow news day at Elland Road. Sometimes, just sometimes, James can remember what things were like before life at Leeds became a soap opera after 'living the dream'. He now combines freelance writing with teaching English in Bradford.

INTRODUCTION: DIGGING UP THE PAST

BY RICK BROADBENT

I dug up my dad around the time Leeds were getting crap again, although I should stress that was a coincidence. Mum was moving south by necessity after a life spent in Yorkshire and her sons had already gone, for love and money. So, on a sad, wet day we turned up to Tadcaster cemetery and, not having exhumed a loved one before, forgot to bring a casket. The man from the cemetery went to get a coffee pot and started shovelling in the coagulated ashes.

'Do you want it all?' he asked.

'Well, as much as you can manage,' I said, with a glance at Mum.

The idea was to take him to Lamorna Cove in Cornwall and scatter the ashes in a place he loved. And we did, throwing a shot of Scotch into the container before we did the deed, and then going for a drink of our own at the Wink, one of those unwelcoming pubs stained brown and with snaggle-toothed locals drinking from personalised tankards, sitting on personalised stools, taking it all personally.

I mention this because it was the end of my immediate family's physical links with Yorkshire, but it's true what they say – you can take the man out of Yorkshire, even when he has been dead for years, uproot him from God's own country and then chuck him off a cliff, nearly decapitating seagulls as he goes, but you can't ever take the Yorkshire out. Now that Dad is gone from that tiny plot in Taddy cemetery Elland Road is my place of remembrance, and so I watch Leeds and think of sitting in the North-East stand all those years ago. I was 17 when my dad died but it is a comfort to know we will always have Ray Hankin. The further away those days get the more I cherish them.

Football is mainly about family – your own one where allegiances and stories are passed down, and the bigger, communal one. Like all families, you fall out, slam doors, say you 'hate' them and then realise you love them more than any third-round FA Cup exit. They say you don't choose your family, but I did. I was born in Leeds, but outside our house in a village called Stutton was a rusty signpost that said 'York 11 miles, Leeds 12'. Well, they could bugger off if they thought I was committing to a life at Bootham Crescent.

Leeds were about to fade when I started watching them, even though they got to the European Cup final that year. I loved it. The noise, the madness, the edge, Tony Currie . . . especially Tony Currie. Leeds always make me think of my dad, which is probably how it should be, and despite the almost unremitting misery of recent times, I'm grateful for that.

All fans think their own club unique, but Leeds really are. Being Leeds we always have to defend ourselves, a status underlined by the furore that followed *The Damned Utd* and the exhuming of the 1970s. We are Leeds and we know you are still laughing but we have got bonds forged from white shirts, purple trackies, sock tags, yacht tax, carpet bowls, the tallest floodlights in Europe, starry nights in Europe, Stuttgart and bans from Europe, Ronnie Hilton, smiley badges, golden memories, ginger midfielders, the odd cut, lots of bruises, '72, '74, '90, '92.

There is now a generation growing up who do not know a Leeds other than the one that has made an art form out of messing with your hope before putting it back in mid-table. I still wonder what might have happened if they had made the Champions League that year when Peter Ridsdale gambled the future on a dream. In truth, I probably knew things were amiss when I interviewed him for *The Times* in the offices of Miss World in Soho Square amid stories of rented goldfish. He said the reason he bought Robbie Keane was because he never thought Robbie Fowler would become available, so when he did he bought him too. It did not sound a foolproof system.

But part of being a Leeds fan is suffering. It is why those rare highs – the win down at Bournemouth to gain promotion back to the top flight; that bizarre title-decider at Sheffield United; beating AC Milan; beating Man United – are so emotional.

This first volume of interviews and essays dips into the highs and lows of being a Leeds fan. I'm biased but I think we have got a great team who have chosen great subjects. It is intended to celebrate Leedsness but not airbrush the horrors, because that has made us too: always hopeful but with the right to be very bitter about it. So while Noel Whelan gives a wonderful heartfelt appreciation of what it is like to make it for your club (and then be sold by them), I am glad Brian Deane does not skirt the racism that once plagued Elland Road, and that we get a new appreciation of just what Eddie Gray faced when he took charge during the worst of the hooligan years. I think we get a real insight into the changing room and how times have changed since Mick Jones decided to finish the weekly shop as Don Revie sped to his house to sign him. For all those newbie football fans, there is also plenty to prove that Leeds and Man United is still the rivalry, even if it is technically dormant, but you can rejoice in a detailed appraisal of the 1-0 FA Cup win at Old Trafford from those involved. Club favourites – John Charles, Jesus Christ and David Batty – are covered with fresh eyes; myths are debunked. There is a lot of drama, a lot of honesty and eye-watering detail about being pinned against a changing-room wall and called a fucking prima donna.

I have been lucky to meet lots of sports stars through work, but while interviewing people like Bobby Charlton, Mike

Tyson, Usain Bolt and Rory McIlroy has been fun, I did not feel the boyish thrill I had when I sat in Johnny Giles' house in Birmingham as his wife served me tea and toast, or the time I was talking to Peter Lorimer in his pub and John Charles walked in. I don't think I will ever look at a footballer with the same affection I had for Currie and then, for different reasons, David Batty.

Ah, Batty. He percolates through these pages because I think he pretty much sums up Leeds. How we loved the way he reacted when he missed his penalty for England in the shoot-out at the World Cup against Argentina in 1998.

'Yes or no?' Brain Moore, the commentator, asked Kevin Keegan, a question he regretted forever after. Gary Neville, generously, said he expected Batty to score. 'But five minutes from the end I was looking around the pitch thinking, "I can't see any natural penalty takers out here,"' he added, as a caveat. Neville was sixth on the list but was spared that horror. Back in England Batty's father had no doubts about his son's capabilities as he watched the drama unfold on television. 'I knew he would miss even before he took it,' he said.

Batty took it stoically. No collapsing to his knees like Pearce, no tears like Southgate. Batty just poked out his tongue, winced a little and walked back to the halfway line. Afterwards he went over the kick with the bluff honesty Leeds fans loved. 'I was really confident,' he said, 'even though it was the first penalty I had taken since I was a kid.' A man bereft of pizzazz did not bother with a pizza ad.

In the summer of 2018, as Southgate led England into the World Cup, it became clear how deeply his own penalty miss for England had hurt and haunted him. Not Batty. It was the same when he talked about his heart problem. It was, to him, no problem. Since he retired Batty has lived a quiet life away from football.

Noel Whelan explains here just how good Batty was at finishing, but it was the way he played as much as what he did. It was thrillingly no-frills. Many years ago I wrote: 'To understand the importance of David Batty, you really have to come from Yorkshire. He is the perfect synthesis of Briggate, Tetley's Bitter, sooty black buildings, Alan Bennett and a timeline of hard men including Bobby Collins, Billy Bremner and Johnny Giles. His game matches the Yorkshire personality. Short no-nonsense passes. An inherent lack of flair. This is real Yorkshire.'

Leeds United are an enduringly fascinating football club. It is in the blood. We love Leeds even if, at times, we don't much like them. They are good and bad and ugly. At the time of writing Leeds have a new manager, Marcelo Bielsa. I have just watched the first half of the first game of the season and it was better than anything in the last decade, but who knows how this will go, or whether Bielsa will still be here by the time this book makes it to the shelves? This is Leeds and it could be anything – except smooth.

1

All fans love a hometown hero, but **Noel Whelan** had real talent to boot, making his Premier League debut as a teenager in 1993. He was so passionate about his rise and what the club meant to him that we ended up giving him two chapters in this volume. In the first he details what 'living the dream' was really about, away from boardrooms, culminating in an epic FA Youth Cup final against Manchester United.

NOEL WHELAN, PART ONE: DOG SHIT BOY

BY ADAM POPE

Noel Whelan started life growing up in Burmantofts, Leeds, where he quickly became known by the less than glamorous moniker 'Dog Shit Boy'. This was because once, during a fight with some lads, rather than pick up the stone or stick that was lying on the ground in front of him he grabbed a dried turd to throw at his attackers. In the time-honoured tradition of kids showing no mercy a nickname was born.

Whether that prompted the family's move to Headingley is up for debate, but what is undisputed is that is where Whelan began his metamorphosis from Dog Shit Boy to Leeds United cult hero. 'I lived right outside the rugby ground, bang opposite on St Michael's Lane,' he says. 'It's where my folks still live now. So I was very much into rugby league rather than football at the time. I actually started off playing rugby league. I was a Leeds Rhinos fan or, as it was at the time, simply Leeds Rugby League. I was a mascot for a number of years and I would travel to each away game with the wives of Kevin Dick and John Holmes, two players. It was only when I went to Spring Bank Primary School, just outside of Headingley, that I decided football was my game.

'Rugby was tough. I was very, very poorly for a while when I was about seven after catching my first up 'n' under at one of the evening training sessions. The ball was up in the air that long that all the first-team rugby players stopped to watch me as I gathered myself underneath this missile that was coming down at a blistering rate of knots into my arms. The ball had reached such a height that I actually fell on my bum when it finally crashed down to earth. We played touch-and-pass at the time, so I just picked myself back up and started running at the players. I got tagged and there was a big round of applause.

'Sadly, that was not the end of it. The previous night I'd been to a bonfire night do in Roundhay, where I'd swallowed some mercury from the glow bands that you got. It was a luminous yellow glow necklace and I bit into it, not thinking it would make me poorly, but believing that maybe it would give me special powers. Maybe I'd glow in the dark, or something. Well, it didn't work. That evening after training I went to get up and walk and I realised my joints were twisting round. I went to the hospital and my body was bleeding internally. All in the same day – I went from such a high to a massive, crushing low.

'That glow band sent me the direct opposite way to what I'd hoped. Far from having new super-powers I was very, very ill and, when I came out of hospital, that was it – I never really returned to playing rugby.

'I went back to Spring Bank Primary after a month and a half on a drip, having a tube put down my throat at Leeds General Infirmary children's ward and being woken up every day at 6 a.m. to be given hot milk. I despise hot milk now and I despised it then too. It was more a case of, "No, you're all right. Just let me kip, please!"

'So I came back to Spring Bank and I remember lots of "Welcome Back" messages on the blackboard and I just nestled into things. I started playing my football and got really heavily into it. I was always into my sport and I just switched – you didn't get much time with rugby league at primary school anyway.

'I was one of those annoying kids who was kind of good at everything. So I started playing football more regularly and didn't much bother with rugby league. I'd go and watch the games, as I still do now, but I realised I had a talent with a football which carried through into middle school at Beckett

Park and then to Lawnswood School, where I was playing for the sixth form when I was still in the third year. I was playing with 19-year-olds when I was 12 or 13, but I'd always done that anyway when we used to play football around my house and at Hyde Park, where we would put bricks down for the goals.

'Nine times out of ten I'd be by myself in the rugby car park at Headingley, kicking the ball against the barriers, where it would come off the railings at different angles as I did volleys and half-volleys. Lots of games took place in that car park. I had great times there with all my friends and lads who'd just be walking the streets and would challenge us to a game of football. You don't see it much these days as times have changed but they were some of my best childhood memories – football, cricket, rugby and even American Football on the ground itself.

'I used to break in to watch the rugby league and nick the rugby balls off the top of the stand after the games. Up the spiral staircase, up the ladder, on top of the roof where there were holes everywhere so you had to stick to where the metal girders and barriers were. Then I'd throw the balls down over the other side, down into the car park. I'd get white turps to rub the "RLFC" off so I could take them to school and sell them. That's how I got my pocket money, apart from a milk or paper round, a little bit of extra spenders.

'My earliest memories were at the rugby league ground, in the social club and in the car park that used to be the training ground, next to the train track. I had some great times in that car park . . . but some of them are best left there!

'The football gathered pace too. I went for trials with Leeds City Boys and was top scorer at under-11s, 12s and 13s, but it was when you got to 14 and 15 that things started taking shape. My dad, who was a policeman, would take me to Weetwood Police Station and Carnegie College at night, so pretty much every evening I'd be doing weights and reps in the police gym. I'd go to Carnegie and do 100-metre sprints and then 50-metre sprints, then run up hills from the bottom to the top of the grass banking. I didn't really have a social life from 13 to 15 years of age, that stage when you start finding girls attractive. They'd be going out after school on a Friday night, sitting by the church where I'd see them as I'd pass by in the car. They'd be laughing and joking, drinking alcohol illegally. That was very frowned upon by myself, I must say. I'd come back from a massive session doing running and being pushed in a gym doing reps, so I felt a bit left out seeing my friends with the girls that I liked. I didn't really have much of a childhood when it came to that sort of stuff. I was too busy training, with my dad pushing me in the gym and at Carnegie, where I'd be doing stupid hill runs. He had an accident and was paralysed from the waist down when I was nine to 13, so maybe he was making up for that. I'd get to my tenth hill run and he'd challenge me to beat my first time, which was ridiculous. He would be at the top timing me. He took me to loads of parks, just me and him, all sorts of places around Leeds.

'I'd always get a new football and boots for Christmas and my dad, fit again, would spend hours just crossing balls for me to volley or head. I'd go and fetch the balls because there were no nets, so it took a lot longer. I forfeited a lot as a kid in terms of those social evenings with my friends, and I resented it. I wanted a little of that normal life for myself as well, but I never got it. My childhood was spent in the gym, bench pressing, doing sit-ups, running laps around the gym, up the hills, 100 metres, 400 metres. I was a natural athlete and I enjoyed the challenge, but I knew you only get one childhood. I suppose in the long run it probably worked out for the best.

'I always knew I had something when we played in the car parks. I would be running rings around people, older boys and young men who were seven years older than this 12-year-old kid. That's why I always enjoyed the physical side of the game because when you do that to an older person they don't take it well. You learn fast. I took a couple of kicks and a couple of knocks. You get used to that. But you also challenge yourself to keep showing them up because you know it's getting to them. I wasn't daunted by playing against men. They were a lot more physically developed, but their skills weren't.

'At Leeds City Boys I realised I was doing very well all the way through to 15, when you get the scouts looking at you from different football clubs. So I had Everton looking at me, I had Arsenal looking at me. Man United looked at me and I went there for trials. The only team that never looked at me was the only one I wanted: Leeds. They were in the league below then, the old Division Two. I was very close to signing for Everton because I thought Leeds were never actually going to come in, even though the players who were at Leeds City Boys and who were getting trials weren't as good as me.

'I always questioned my dad, "Why haven't they come in for me?" I guess they thought I wouldn't have signed for them, but I'm a homegrown boy, a Leeds United supporter. It got to me. I found it very puzzling. So I was very close to signing for Everton at 16, but they wanted me to finish my last year of school in Liverpool and I didn't fancy that. I'm a home-bird. I love coming back, I love being near my family, I love being back in Leeds. Even today when I bring my daughter with me, we see the skyline of Leeds on the M1 and then, as you come into the city, there's a little gap in the trees and there, you see it . . . you're home.

'I think my dad wanted me to do whatever made me happy. Finally, after what seemed for ever, Leeds did come in and I got schoolboy forms with them. I passed that year and then signed a two-year YTS, but I was really close to missing out because they were playing me at centre-half for some reason, even though I'd been top scorer for Leeds City Boys for four years!

'It was a coach called Peter Gunby who put me there because I had just shot up suddenly. I was always short and stocky but then all of a sudden I'd got a little bit of height on me and the rest of me hadn't grown into it. I was still quite lanky at the time. They said I wasn't the same player. I said, "That's because you are not playing me up front." In the end it was only the latter stages of that schoolboy year where they played me up top, and I started banging goals in.

'So I signed my two-year YTS on the pitch at Elland Road with Rob Bowman and the manager, Howard Wilkinson, before a game. They said they were taking a chance on me. I didn't care. I was absolutely over the moon, ecstatic, a Leeds boy with an opportunity with a football club I love.

'At the time I went to the games and watched the likes of David Rennie, Mark Aizlewood, Scott Sellars, David Batty, Gary Speed and Brendan Ormsby. We also had Ian Baird up front. All these players with "Lion Cabinets" on their shirts playing in the Zenith Data Systems Cup. I'd seen them in my Junior Whites scarf as a Leeds United supporter after I'd got the P52 bus from town to the ground with my brother. I liked them all but Speedo and Batty were the two players I absolutely adored from the stands. To me they were what Leeds epitomised at the time. Loads of heart, loads of passion, loads of skill, and they were kind of like my heroes. So I ran in and said, "I want to clean your boots," and from the very first day we got a good relationship going because they could see my enthusiasm and my potential.

'Christmas would come and I'd get my tips. I'd make sure their ASICS were nicely cleaned. I'd spit on them so the white bits showed up better. I did extra around the ground to help out more. It was a very disciplined outfit at the time when you were a YTS. It wasn't like what we have nowadays. Far from it – it was a lot tougher. I had to clean the toilets. I had to clean the brass where you pissed on, get it shining, so I had to get the polish right in where it had turned purple from people doing their business every day. I had to clean all the sprayed piss up too. Then I had to clean the first-team dressing room and the manager's room, clean all their boots and hang the kits out. I had to make sure I was in earlier than everyone else to make sure the kits were ready. Howard Wilkinson was always pushing me. He'd make me clean his car – nobody else, just me. He had a Lexus and he'd make me clean it inside and out. You can't say no to the gaffer, but I was like, "Why me? What have I done?"

'Looking back from the outside, all these years on, he probably wanted to instil a little more discipline into me as a person. I was lively and more outspoken than most – because I knew I had ability and I was always confident like that. Some people are naturally a bit shyer, but I was quite an open fella and if I had something to say then I'd say it even though I shouldn't. Howard Wilkinson's way of managing that was to push me further than he did the other players.

'We would have what we called court cases. If someone wasn't cleaning the top of the pipes properly in the dressing room then Paul Hart, the academy manager, would have a court session on a Sunday at 7 a.m., not long after we'd all got in at 3 a.m. from a big night out. Once, we had to be at Elland Road for that time, but the gates were closed and we were left standing outside in the cold for two hours wondering where Harty was. It turned out he was still at home. He rang the security guard at the ground to come out and give us a message from the gaffer: "Right you lot can fuck off now." We're all stood there lagging from the night before, sweating out beer. It was very hard. Sometimes we'd give each other a court case too. Punishments included standing naked while people took wire brushes to the back of your legs and back. Sometimes we'd strip the guilty player and hang him naked from the crossbar while we fired balls at him. Another thing we did was called "Lights Out". In those days there were thick metal coat-hooks that you'd hang the kit on. If anyone let us down in any way we'd stick them in the first-team dressing room after the players had gone home. The lights would be turned off and you'd pick a corner to hide in. Everyone would then file in and lob these metal hangers around, hoping they would hit the offender. You just covered yourself up the best you could. Or sometimes you'd just have a naked, one-on-one fight. Things like that. It was tough.

'I remember one time we gave the goalkeeper Paul Pettinger a court case. We tied him up naked at the top of the training ground at Fullerton. There was a little five-a-side football pitch there on the concrete and he was bound up with skipping ropes around his body, arms, back and neck. We volleyed balls at him from seven yards and one hit him full pelt in the face and knocked him clean out. He began choking on the skipping rope so we had to help him up. The ambulance came and Paul Hart went absolutely ballistic. So that one kind of went wrong. After that the old skipping rope went out of the window, but we carried on with everything else.

'Paul Hart was good but hard. He was fair, he was honest and he'd say it how it was. You appreciate that more as you get older. My first coming together with him was when I was doing a BTEC at Thomas Danby College in Chapeltown. I'd get the bus down from Headingley with some of the Leeds Rugby League players of the time and their academy players. The classroom at the college had a polystyrene ceiling and, when the teacher went out of the room during one lesson, I began throwing a stick up at it. I was shocked when the whole roof came down, not just one square, the lot. It was impossible to keep that quiet.

'I was sent back to Paul Hart's office, which was actually a little Portakabin. I walked up the stairs to it and as soon as I entered, his hand was around my throat: "What the fuck are you playing at, you fucking prima donna!"

'Him calling me a prima donna has always stuck in my mind. Always. Although at the time I didn't know what one was – at first I thought he'd called me "Maradona". I thought, "What a compliment that is, but then why has he got his hand around my throat?" That's the first time I realised that he'd worked with first-team players before he'd come here. It was a tough school with Paul. He was disciplined but he was also a great coach and a great guy. When I was choosing whether to play for England or Ireland, he was the one who pushed me towards

England. He took me to my first game at Lilleshall, which I think was against Nigeria, when I played against the under-16s and 17s in a friendly. I stayed at his house in Nottingham and came back to train the next day. But that day when I was pinned up against his wall, wondering what "prima donna" meant, that was the day I realised I had to start doing things the right way.

'We made it to the FA Youth Cup final in my second year as a YTS. I was playing centre-forward alongside Gary Kelly, who then went to right-back where he became a club stalwart for years. We signed Kevin Sharp and Jamie Forrester from Auxerre. Mark Tinkler also came in. They'd all been given pro contracts as part of the deal to get them to Leeds United. They had that comfort whereas I didn't. I had to work for my pro deal.

'My YTS pay was £17 per week and we came out with nothing at all. So when Christmas came and you got your bonus off Speedo and Batts for looking after their boots and kit, it always made the holiday that bit nicer.

'But it irritated me when others were getting on. They got their pro contracts and I didn't understand why. It's not until you get a little bit older that you realise how football works.

'During my YTS David Batty and me would come in earlier than anyone else. We would probably spend a good hour crossing balls for each other and volleying. We'd take two bags out with us before any of the other YTS or first-team players got there. By the time they arrived and were in the changing rooms it looked like we'd already done a whole training session. We were sweating and just having fun with the football. And, by the way, Batts could finish. He should have scored more goals than he did. He was hitting volleys as sweet as anybody – your Glenn Hoddles and your Kevin Keegans of this world – and everything would hit the back of the net. But because of the job he was required to do he never really found himself in that final third and so he didn't get the opportunity. The fact is he was probably one of the best finishers I've ever seen.

'I practised hard and there weren't many kinds of finishes that I couldn't do. I used to picture things in my mind the night before games, put scenarios in my head ready for the next day so, if it did happen, I'd have an idea of how I was going to turn, if I was going to do a trick, how I was going to score. A lot of it was instinctive. You have those moments where it's bit like a *déjà vu*. It's like you've already thought about it before it happens. That always helped me.

'I was excited by that run to the FA Youth Cup final and I thought endlessly about my game the night before. What will I do if this cross comes in? How do I get across the man? Will it be an overhead kick? It's the things you put into your mind and then go, "Wow, weird, that actually happened."

'Every second I spent training by myself, kicking a ball against a wall, doing overhead kicks and putting more balls through my parents' greenhouse windows in the garden, all of that had all amounted to me becoming the player that I was. But every step on the way to the final had got progressively harder. I remember Sheffield Wednesday at Hillsborough because I wore Eric Cantona's boots. He had just left and I was first in one morning so I raided his shelf and took all these Nikes – they sponsored him at the time. I was excited, thinking that wearing Eric's boots might elevate my game to another level. Just like that, I decided, "Ooh, I'll wear Eric's boots tonight." It was the first time I'd tried them on and I got terrible blisters. That was my second run in with Paul Hart, because I had to come off as I was struggling so much. It was a silly, starry-eyed mistake. Not so much "prima donna" this time but more "you fucking idiot".

'We scraped by Norwich in the semi-final and then it was Man United. You couldn't have got two teams in that era with such a big rivalry. It was a huge sell-out for both legs, because of the hype of Leeds playing Man United for a trophy. Both atmospheres were incredible. Yes, Man United had the names – Beckham, Scholes, the Nevilles. They also had Nicky Butt, Keith Gillespie, Robbie Savage and Ben Thornley. All of them were top players and most of them went on to play for England, Wales or Northern Ireland. But the one thing that had never happened to them was playing a team like us. We were a different breed, a different animal altogether.

"You want to fight us?"

"We're better than you at that."

"You think you're fitter than us?"

"We're way better than you at that because we work tirelessly. We are aggressive and we are fit. It's the Leeds United way."

"You want to play football against us?"

"Well, here's a surprise: we ain't a bad side either. So if you can't beat us in any way then how will you beat us home and away?"

'The first game at Old Trafford: it was dark and packed. There was tension and nerves, as you'd expect – a raw excitement. I remember going past Chris Casper and then the keeper as he came charging out. I took it round him and slipped it through into the goal – just brilliant. You're in a two-legged final and it's Man United, out of the darkness, under the lights. But, you know, I didn't really celebrate that much. I was just overjoyed. I have to say my celebrations all the way through my career were pretty shit. It was just a "*Yes!*" I never had anything planned, so it was just a natural reaction, the way it should be. Scoring any goal at any level is always a pleasure. You ask almost any kid what's the best feeling they've had? It's scoring a goal. It's just some strange type of adrenalin which rushes through your body, and so anything you may have had planned, like any type of stupid dance, just goes out of the window.

'Everything just took over that night. We left them sprawled out on the floor, literally, three or four red-shirted bodies lying around Old Trafford. They'd never met such a fit, talented and aggressive bunch of players that could also play football. They'd not met a Leeds United on the way to the final and it must have been a massive eye-opener to them. We won the first leg 2-1. We had given ourselves a great opportunity for the second leg at Elland Road, but we didn't expect what awaited us when we walked out to another full house at home. We expected it to be filled to the rafters, but the noise was simply incredible. It still gets me now every single time I think about it. In the tunnel the first thing we saw was the Lowfields terrace, rammed all the way along. Then we came out to "Marching on Together". It's a sight we'd only normally see as a ball boy when you're watching the first team, but all of a sudden it was happening to us. We were the ones playing and the first team were watching. It was like role reversal but with the same atmosphere and the same crowd against Man United – we're the first team and they're us, for one night only.

'I was one of the few Leeds lads there, along with Matty Smithard, Kevin Daly and Alex Byrne, who were in the Leeds City Boys with me. We had a really good squad of young local lads and imports like Mark Tinkler from the north-east and Jamie Forrester from Blackpool. Whatever our geographical backgrounds we just had a togetherness about us and a strength of mind as a team. I think that meant they were never ever going to contain us. There was a lot of pressure on me, being a Leeds boy, playing at Elland Road in a final, knowing it was probably one of my last big games before being offered a pro contract. I'd scored 32 goals that year already. Jamie got 33 so beat me by one, but if you ask him how many I set up for him and how many he had set up for me there'd be a massive difference. He was a greedy little sod.

'That night I set up both goals. Once again Chris Casper and the other centre-half, who I don't remember, couldn't deal with me. I was too good, too strong, too physical and had too much energy. It was a massive culture shock to them. They couldn't match us. Yes, they had talent, no doubt about that, but when you've got somebody in your face for 90 minutes, not allowing you to play your game, leaving you on your backside every two minutes, challenging for every ball, well, it can't have been nice. And they weren't the first team we'd done that to that season. We battered teams.

'Jamie scored the first with an overhead kick. That made it 3-1 on aggregate and we thought we were there. Scholes equalised on the night but then I flicked on a ball almost instantly and Matty Smithard scored. The fact was we'd got a real cushion before half-time and we'd also hurt them, and I mean physically hurt them. We emulated the first team by being fit but being quality too. You had to be fitter than everybody else, and I was probably fitter than most of the first team. I would do the runs and I would win by minutes, not seconds. I enjoyed being an athlete. That was part of my game.

'I know the Man United players were gutted because I went on the England under-18s' camp afterwards with Gary Neville, and it was clear they couldn't get it out of their system. They were still talking about it and I'd just sit there and say, "Dry your eyes, your dad's called Neville Neville."

'We walked up and got the Cup in the West Stand at Elland Road. It was just the best feeling in the world. I looked across at Mum, Dad, my cousins. Everyone was there. Straight out into town afterwards. I can remember up to a certain point and then everything is just a blank. I do remember leaving my car at Elland Road and I don't think I picked it up for a couple of days. It was the best feeling, the best moment, because you're wearing a badge you have supported all your life. It was probably more special to me and the Leeds boys than it was to anybody else. I had started out as Dog Shit Boy. Now look at me. I love my football but there's something about being a homegrown lad and winning stuff that means that much more.'

2

The ultimate unsung hero. Google "Mick Jones" and you will probably end up reading about The Clash guitarist. Failing that, the Foreigner guitarist. But **Mick Jones** was pivotal to Leeds' one truly great team in the late 1960s and early 1970s. Allan Clarke got the limelight, but Jones was the grafter, born in mining country and digging Leeds out of many a hole with 77 goals in 200 games. This fascinating interview sheds new light on a man best remembered for the 1972 FA Cup final when he climbed the steps with his arm in a sling. Of course, Clarke scored the winner and he best summed up Jonah's brilliance when he told me: 'The only thing that disappoints me is we never played for England together. When I got in the England side I played with them all – Jimmy Greaves, Peter Osgood, Geoff Hurst, but never Jonah. And make no mistake: we were the most feared partnership in Europe.'

MICK JONES: ARE YOU IN PAIN?'

BY PHIL HAY

On the Monday after he signed for Leeds United Mick Jones and his wife Glenis took a stroll along Briggate in the centre of Leeds. A one-time medieval market, the city's main drag was an attractive collection of Victorian and Edwardian architecture, an eye-opener for a footballer who grew up in mining country on the border between Yorkshire and Nottinghamshire. Jones was an unassuming sort but instantly recognisable to anyone who had read the weekend's newspapers. Somewhere along the street he was accosted by a group of women. 'Oh,' gasped one, giving him a hug. 'I want to know what £100,000 feels like!'

Jones was not *au fait* with money like that and neither were Leeds United. The striking aspect of Don Revie's empire at Elland Road was how few transfer fees were needed to build it. A giveaway price of £33,000 was agreed with Manchester United for Johnny Giles in 1963. Allan Clarke was the big exception, joining from Leicester City for £165,000 six years later. Clarke's move broke the British transfer record and a £100,000 deal for Jones, arriving from Sheffield United in September of 1967, was not far short of doing the same. A year earlier Everton had set a new mark by signing Alan Ball from Blackpool for £112,000. When it came to scouting players, Revie preferred to find them young and create household names for a nominal outlay but on rare occasions the cheque book came out. For two years he pursued Jones, keen to buy the bustling centre-forward

but unable to force his way through Sheffield United's door.
Revie wore a look of relief when Jones, sat at his own living-
room table, signed a contract with Leeds worth £70 a week. 'He
told me he'd been after me for two years. "What a nightmare it's
been trying to get this done," he said. It was news to me. I had
no idea, none whatsoever.'

In the only transfer of his career, Jones was the last to know.
Professional football had been a blessing for him, a lifestyle he
was grateful for, and the idea of leaving Bramall Lane was not
his. Jones had come to Sheffield United by way of a successful
trial, offered to him after he was spotted playing for Dinnington
Miners' Welfare in a local South Yorkshire league. Coal mining
ran in the family for Jones. His father worked in the collieries
for 50 years and his childhood was spent in the pit village of
Shireoaks, a short distance west of Worksop. On Saturdays he
and his father would travel together to watch whichever of
the Sheffield clubs was playing at home. Wednesday one week,
United the next; Hillsborough or Bramall Lane depending on
the fixture list. 'He was a massive football fan but he'd never say
much to me about the football I played,' Jones says. 'He went to
every match from me being 11 years old at school. Everywhere
I went, he was there. But he never said much. He kept out of it
and let me get on with it. I don't think he wanted to interfere. I
don't think he wanted to be pushy.'

By the age of 15 Jones had taken a job at Carlton Cycles in
Worksop, pushing himself through 50 hours of manual labour
a week. 'I'd been there ten months and I hated it. It was a job,
and it was good to have a job, but I loved football and I wanted
to play football.' When the offer of a trial at Sheffield United
was made, Jones jumped at it. On Tuesday nights and Thursday
nights a development squad of sorts trained under the lights
at Bramall Lane, angling for apprentice forms. Among the
aspiring footballers who shared the pitch with Jones was a
young Howard Wilkinson, soon to join Sheffield Wednesday.

'One evening they put this match on in front of John Harris, the manager, and the rest of the Sheffield United staff,' Jones says. 'They were always there looking for talent, seeing what we could do. The match finished 6-4 and we lost but I scored all four goals. I came off ringing with sweat thinking, "I enjoyed that." And as I did I saw this guy in a Trilby walking towards me. It was the assistant manager, Archie Clark. He said, "Now then, son, where do you work?" I said, "I work at Worksop, Mr Clark, at Carlton Cycles." He said, "You'll not be working there next week. I want you to come and sign as an apprentice." I was speechless. It happened that quickly. The club got in touch with my work and I was told to be there first thing on Monday morning, down at Bramall Lane.'

Jones' day job was paying him one pound 11 shillings a week. Sheffield United upped his wage to five pounds, enough for Jones to pay his mother a pound a week for the upkeep of the house. Harris, a Glaswegian who had played for Chelsea as a centre-half in the post-war years, quickly warmed to Jones' intelligence and craft: robust, terrier-like, powerful in the air and savvy when it came to goalscoring. Four days before his 18th birthday in April 1963, Jones made his first-team debut away to Matt Busby's Manchester United. The surprise at seeing the line-up for Old Trafford was not unlike that felt by Jack Charlton prior to his debut for Leeds a decade earlier. Charlton, an amusing after-dinner speaker, tells the story of John Charles leaning over his shoulder, pointing at Charlton's name on the senior teamsheet and asking, quite genuinely, 'Who the fuck's that?'

'In those days they put all the different teams up in the dressing room,' Jones says. 'I was in the reserves at the time and I'd scored nine goals in nine games. I looked at the reserve team and thought, "I'm not playing. He's dropped me! How can that be?" Then one of the lads shouts, "Mick, have a look at the first team. You're at Man United tomorrow." It was a shock. I was only 17. I thought, "Christ, this'll be an eye-opener."'

Sheffield United drew 1-1 at Old Trafford and were back in Manchester the following week, winning 3-1 at Manchester City. Jones scored twice. Another goal followed against Leyton Orient and another against Tottenham Hotspur; four in the last six games of the season: 'I felt I'd done well and it was a good bit of experience. I'd made a start and the next season I went straight into the first team. That was it. I was away.'

Jones' name and reputation did not take long to get around. Later, around the time of his transfer to Leeds, he discovered that Manchester United, Arsenal and Tottenham were all as interested in signing him as Revie, and had been trying to do so without success.

In 1965, aged 20 and one year out from the World Cup, a letter from the Football Association was handed to him in the dressing room at Bramall Lane. Sir Alf Ramsey had named him in the England squad for a clutch of three friendlies, the second against Germany in Nuremberg. Sheffield United, who were heading to New Zealand on tour, travelled without him. Jones was honoured but immediately felt out of his comfort zone. 'International players are very cliquey,' he says. 'You don't really know them or you only know them from playing against them for your club. You had the Londoners in a clique together – Jimmy Greaves, Bobby Moore and co. They'd be in one group and others would stick together too. I found it quite lonely, not like Leeds, where it felt like being in a family. International players play for themselves, I think. That's how I saw it. So before the Germany game I was on my own on the training pitch, fiddling with the ball in the goalmouth. I noticed Sir Alf Ramsey walking my way. He'd had elocution lessons so he talked rather like this [Jones affects the Queen's English]: "Michael, I have some very good news for you. I'm playing you against Germany tomorrow, congratulations." And that was that. He walked off.'

England beat Germany 1-0. Jones found the net from long range but saw his strike disallowed and Terry Paine, a forward with Southampton, scored the only goal. Ramsey's squad flew on to play Sweden in Gothenburg but Jones, who kept his place, felt jaded and out of sorts. 'I don't know what was wrong with me but for some reason I didn't feel good. I played but I was shattered and I didn't do myself justice.' Jones would not play for England again until 1970, when he met Holland and Johan Cruyff in his pomp. 'My God, could he run,' Jones says. 'He was like lightning that guy.' The game at Wembley, a 0-0 draw, was Jones' third and final cap.

Where England were concerned, Jones was a victim of competition in an era of fine domestic forwards: Greaves, Geoff Hurst and, latterly, Allan Clarke. But at club level he was sought after, and Harris knew it. 'There were clubs interested but John had put the block on it all,' Jones says. 'He wouldn't tell you anything, not unless you really pushed him. The same happened to Alan Woodward, one of my teammates there. He wanted away but couldn't get a move. But I wasn't unhappy at Sheffield United. I was playing and doing my best, earning £35 a week, plus four pounds for a win or two pounds for a draw. It was good enough for me, but still, I was fortunate to find out about Leeds trying to sign me because going there was the best thing I ever did. Honestly, I was the last person who knew about it.'

Jones was tipped off by Joe Shaw, a wise old pro who was very near the end of his career. 'I looked up to Joe,' Jones says. 'He was getting on but what a player he'd been. We were going through our exercises this Friday morning and out of the blue he says to me, "Here, Mick, you ought to get yourself off to Leeds. Sixty quid a week you'll get there. Get yourself gone." He told me Leeds were after me and I said, "Are they?" That's how little I knew. A little later I got myself down to the ground and went to ask John Harris directly. He talked about the club getting a few enquiries but wouldn't say what was actually happening. I was thinking, "Just give me an answer." Eventually I got the chairman, Dick Wragg, on the phone and I told him I had to think about my career. He took that in and promised me that Leeds would be in touch later that afternoon. In a couple of hours I went from being totally unaware to having Don Revie round at my house.'

Jones had no agent or representatives and, in the meantime, life went on. On Fridays he and his wife were in the habit of doing their weekly shop at a supermarket in nearby Dinnington. Revie was on his way south, but they stuck to their routine regardless, doing a double-take as Leeds United's manager zipped past them in a Ford Zephyr. The memories of it bring out hysterical laughter in Jones. 'My wife says, "Hey, there's Don Revie going past." But, and I can't believe this now, we carried on and got the shopping as usual. When we drove back into the estate there was this bizarre scene with all this scaffolding built up outside our house. TV cameras were there to film me and Don was waiting in the street. I took him in and made him a cup of tea.'

Negotiations, as Jones recalls them, took all of five minutes. Revie asked if he was ambitious, to which Jones replied that he was. He asked about money and Jones played it straight. 'It never crossed my mind to tell him I was earning 60 quid a week. I was dead honest and told him Sheffield United were paying me £35. "I'll double it," he said. And I said, "Give me the pen."'

Revie was a tactician and a strategist, the inventor of before-their-time dossiers detailing the strengths and weaknesses of opposition players. Some in the dressing room warmed to that amount of preparation more than others. To quote Peter Lorimer, 'By the time you'd finished reading you'd think a Third Division full-back was the best player in the world. I used to say to myself, "I don't need this. Just let me go out there and beat the arse off him." But what Jones liked most about Revie, and what he discovered in their first conversation, was his devotion to his players, their families and their well-being. Flowers would arrive when relatives were ill. Golf days were regular events on the calendar, and the players travelled in all the style Revie could offer before away games. 'He was a players' man, not a directors' man,' Jones says. 'The best example I can give is this. We were playing down at Crystal Palace once and in those days we took a train to King's Cross and then a coach to south London. The traffic was always difficult. After the game – we won 2-0 and I scored the second goal – he spotted a couple of the club's directors walking past the bus and heading for a drink. He said, very politely, "Gentleman, I need you back here by 5.30 p.m. and no later than that." We were on the bus playing cards and as time went on we started watching the clock: 5.27, 5.28, 5.29. At half-past, with no sign of the directors, Don turned to the bus driver and said, "Right, off you go." We left them behind. All of us thought he'd be sacked. He'd be gone by next week, we reckoned. But he wasn't because everything he did was right for the team, and the team was more important than anything else.'

Jones' £100,000 price tag was a badge of honour to some, not least the excitable ladies in Briggate, but it carried no weight in Revie's dressing room. By 1967 the squad at Leeds was full of big hitters or soon-to-be big hitters: Giles, Lorimer, Charlton, Norman Hunter and the ball of fire that was Billy Bremner. The club did not do passengers or easy initiations. 'It was a hard dressing room to go into. I found it tough at first with guys like Billy and Gilesy. You were talking about a club with 16 internationals, something like that, and you had to win them over. It didn't really matter who you were or what you'd done before. They wanted you to prove that you were good enough to be there. Once you won them over you found them to be the tightest bunch you could ever find, but you had to be careful going in.'

For years Jones roomed with Paul Madeley, the 'Rolls Royce', as he came to be known. Madeley was the most disciplined member of Revie's squad, immensely fit and professional. 'He never drank, he never smoked and he always looked after himself,' Jones says. 'He's had a lot of health problems recently, and it makes me think there's no justice at all considering what an athlete he was.' (Editor's note – not long after Phil's interview with Mick, we were all sorry to hear of Paul Madeley's death at the age of 73 from complications associated with Parkinson's disease. He is survived by his wife Ann and sons Jason and Nick.)

In the dressing room Jones got the rougher end of the stick, forced to change next to Bremner. The combustive Scot was renowned for his temper but had a sense of humour to match his temperament. 'Talk about piss-taking,' Jones says. 'It was a nightmare in there, a real nightmare with Billy. You had to be careful with what you wore, what you took in there. But we were all for one. The relationship between us seemed to come naturally.'

With unforgiving eyes on him Jones felt the need to start scoring goals quickly. Goals were his currency and he equated confidence with the ability to find the net. He had seen what shattered confidence could do to a player at Sheffield United where Tony Wagstaff, a slight midfielder who would later act as best man at Jones' wedding, had been reduced to tears by the stresses of underperforming and frustrating the crowd. The timing of Jones' introduction at Elland Road was not ideal. He had missed the best part of two weeks of training with Sheffield United and was lacking in fitness. 'I never told anyone that, but six or seven games went by without me scoring, which starts to get you a bit worried,' he says. 'Then, finally, I got my first one against Arsenal and the confidence came back. Goalscoring is all about confidence. You can't explain it to anyone if they've never been there. Get two or three on the trot and you can't wait to get out. If you're not scoring, you dread going onto the pitch.'

Goals had never been a problem at Sheffield United – 63 on his record after 149 league appearances – and before long they came naturally at Leeds. As Jones' stature grew, appreciation of his influence spiralled. With a rugged frame and a mop of red hair he was the club's original cult hero, lacking the flair or magic of a prodigy like Eddie Gray but a lynchpin in a team who knew how to play, how to stick the boot in and how to win. Revie once told Jones, in a quiet moment, that his was consistently the first name on the teamsheet. 'I felt valued,' Jones says. 'I can think back to a day when I was struggling with injury and trying to decide whether to play or not. Billy pipes up, "You better fucking play, Jonah. We need you." That was a compliment. The way I saw it, my position was the hardest position on the pitch. You've got to battle and fight and come up with goals, and if it isn't working the team doesn't work. Look at the years Leeds won the title. Lee Chapman scored most goals in 1992. In 1969 and 1974 I was top goalscorer – not bad for players who weren't the most skilful or the most fashionable.'

He was quickly amongst the trophies at Elland Road: a Fairs Cup medal in 1968, earned by Jones scoring the only goal in the final against Ferencváros (Leeds won the League Cup that same year but Jones was Cup-tied) and the Division One championship the following year. Revie's squad became heavily decorated, though not to the extent which they might have been. The 1969–70 season was a year of near-misses, a year in which Leeds went for everything and came home with nothing, pipped by Chelsea in the FA Cup final, Celtic in the European Cup semi-finals and Everton in the league. An improbable treble asked too much in the end. Jones struck in both the FA Cup final against Chelsea, on a dog of a pitch at Wembley, and again in the replay, but still finished on the losing side. 'What did us in that season, and it wouldn't be allowed to happen now, was the schedule,' he says. 'If the games had been spread out then we might have done it, but we played a few very important matches in the space of about ten days and it was far too much. The FA Cup final was annoying. Of all the people to score the winner in the last minute of the replay, it would be David Webb – who Eddie Gray had taken to the cleaners in both matches. But losing to Celtic was no disgrace. They were the best side I ever played against. Jimmy Johnstone, or "Jinky", as they called him – to see that guy play was mesmerising, almost unbelievable. Terry Cooper was a great full-back and no one ever went past him like Jimmy Johnstone did. TC came into the dressing room after the first leg saying, "I don't want to play against him every week."'

By the start of the 1969–70 season Allan Clarke was on board. He was a singular figure – quiet, withdrawn but a spiky personality – but Clarke and Jones clicked; friends back then and close friends to this day. Clarke, whose finishing earned him the nickname 'Sniffer', was the silkier of the pair, a cultured footballer with a predator's brain. He and Jones dovetailed in a telepathic manner, perfectly suited to each other. 'I was a different type of player,' Jones says. 'You'd call me the bustling type. Good in the air and strong, a physical guy. He had the guile, with some style with his play. "Finesse" is probably the word. We hit it off straight away and he was such a good player. I always found that when you played with good players, you played well yourself. "Telepathic" is a good way to describe what we had, and you don't coach that. It's something that clicks of its own accord. Don knew he wanted an extra piece of the jigsaw putting in, so he spent the money and he got Clarkey. It worked perfectly.'

Jones and Clarke show up in the most replayed ten seconds of Leeds United's history – the footage which captures the only goal in the centenary FA Cup final in 1972. Jones, in typically industrious form, ekes space out of Arsenal left-back Bob McNab and rides a sliding tackle before hooking a cross towards the penalty spot. Sniffer is there and dives to head the ball, beating Geoff Barnett inside his left-hand post.

Clarke, one-nil.

The phrase still echoes at Elland Road.

'You sometimes get partnerships where there's a bit of jealousy,' Jones says. 'One wants to score more than the other, or neither player wants to do the supporting role. We were never like that. I was as happy setting him up to score at Wembley as I would have been scoring myself. We were mates and we've always got on. He can be volatile and he's not everyone's cup of tea, but people don't know him like I know him. He's a generous guy to a fault.'

As long lasting as the images of Clarke's stooping header is the footage of Jones at the end of the final. On his first visit to Wembley in 1970 he found the turf had been destroyed by the Horse of the Year show staged there two weeks earlier. In 1972 the grass was plush to the point of being spongy, like no surface Jones had played on before. 'It was strange, like a thick, plush carpet.' Late in the game he fell and leant heavily on one elbow, sinking into the grass and dislocating it. In agonising pain, Jones was attended to by members of St John Ambulance but ignored their insistence that he depart for the medical room. 'Les Cocker [Revie's assistant] told me to go with them and get proper treatment, but I pointed behind him and said, "No, I'm going up there." With the help of Hunter and his arm in a sling, Jones struggled up Wembley's 39 steps and took his winners' medal from the Queen and the Duke of Edinburgh.

'Any other game, no, I wouldn't have done that, but you dreamt about being there as a kid and I was going up those steps,' Jones says. 'It felt like a million miles and I thought I was a going to be sick, but I didn't want to miss out. My wife was crying as I went past her and Norman's next to me saying, "It's all right, mate, I've got you." I shook hands with the Duke of Edinburgh and he asked me if I was OK. Norman whispered,

"Is he fucking joking?" Then the Queen asked me, "Are you in pain?" and I thought I should be as polite as I could be. "Yes Ma'am, a little."

'Once I'd stood through the national anthem I was taken away, stripped off and laid on a table. The shock had started to kick in. Four doctors who'd been found from nowhere came and put my elbow back in place, two pulling in one direction and two pulling in the other. It was awful. The rest of the players headed off on the coach for a game at Wolves on the Monday. I spent the rest of Saturday in the Royal Gardens Hotel, being physically sick all night.' .

Leeds' league game at Wolverhampton Wanderers, the last of the season and just 48 hours after the FA Cup final, was another travesty of timing. The club needed a point to claim the title and complete the Double but tired and stretched, they lost 2-1. Derby County finished top of the First Division. It was one of several occasions on which Revie's players felt robbed: the infamous defeat to West Brom in 1971 in which referee Ray Tinkler ignored an offside flag and caused a pitch invasion at Elland Road; the 1973 European Cup Winners' Cup final and the 1975 European Cup final, both of which fell foul of inept – and in the case of 1973 – corrupt refereeing. 'Those were major titles which were lost through no fault of our own,' Jones says. 'The Wolves game was torture. I was injured so we drove down on the Monday and it was bumper to bumper on the M1. There were about 20,000 Leeds fans outside Molineux, listening to loud speakers. I was crammed into this little broadcasting box and I could see that the lads weren't right. We were tired and mentally drained, so soon after a Cup final. Wolves had been waiting for us. They kicked hell out of us and they got the result. It was so sad to see the title go that way.'

Jones made it to Paris for the 1975 European Cup final but only as an injured onlooker. Leeds were in unavoidable transition by then and the old guard were retreating. Charlton retired

in 1973 and Revie ended his era the following year, taking the
England job after winning the First Division again. 'He knew
that team was breaking up,' Jones says. 'You can't go on for
ever at that level and he knew it. Some of us were retired and
most of us were getting old. The England job had been offered
and none of us blamed him for taking it, but it was the end of
Leeds United as we knew it.'

Jones had helped Revie sign off with a second league title
but at a cost. Years of wear and tear on his left leg had done
gradual damage to his knee. By the 1973–74 season, a year in
which Leeds went 29 league games unbeaten and Jones scored
14 times, the pain became overwhelming. He discovered a
bursa behind his knee before a game against Sheffield United
but agreed to play for as long as he could. 'Don took me to
one side and said, "We've got six games to win the title. Get
me through these six games." I wasn't about to refuse. He told
me I'd get a nice holiday in the summer and an operation. I
did. I went to Otley Hospital and then tried for 18 months to
get back to normal, but I was never the same. I couldn't jump
like I used to, and I wasn't the sort of guy who was going to sit
around pinching money. So I gave it up.'

Jones' injury was directly related to his style as a centre-
forward. 'I used to jump off the same leg all the time, and if
I'd known what I know now I'd have done things differently.
One of my legs is an inch shorter than the other, which meant
there wasn't enough strength in the shorter one. What I needed
to do was build up my quad muscles to compensate. That's
what you'd do nowadays. All the stress went into that knee and
eventually it cracked a bone.'

Jimmy Armfield, who took the reins at Elland Road after
Revie's replacement, Brian Clough, had come and gone in 44
days, had unexpectedly succeeded in reviving Eddie Gray's
playing career. At the time Gray was waiting for the Football
League's insurers to confirm his retirement, but Jones played in

a series of reserve matches and realised that his time was up. 'I knew I was done,' he says. 'I played for the last time at Elland Road, against Aston Villa's reserves, I think. I didn't play very well and I was conscious all the time of doing more and more damage, worrying that I might cripple myself. I've still got a big scar from where they took the bursa out, and I had to face facts. That was it. I said, "I can't do it any more, I'm finished."' He sat through the 1975 European Cup final and watched a trophy that Revie coveted slip away in a scandalous 2-0 defeat to Bayern Munich. It was, as every player knew, that squad's last chance to win. Lorimer called that night 'the disappointment of our lives'.

Football had given Jones a 12-year career, eight of those at Leeds, but at 30 he retired. Fortunately for him, Giles – then into his thirties himself – had recommended a pension scheme to other players at Elland Road, encouraging them to invest in it.

'Before then there was no such thing,' Jones says. 'You played, you earned your money and then you retired and found another job. When John first spoke to me about it, I really wasn't sure, but it was the best thing that ever happened to a footballer. I took that pension at 31. It wasn't as good as it could have been but I'd have been lost without the money.'

Jones, nonetheless, took to retirement with great difficulty, drifting away from football completely. 'I didn't go to a match for 20 years. It hit me hard, finishing so early, so I kept away. Going to games was like torturing myself over the fact that I couldn't play.' Little by little, work came his way and Sondico, the sportswear brand, employed him as a sales rep in the north of England. The travelling was hard but he stuck with it for seven years, long enough to gain some business acumen and open other doors. When the opportunity arose he bought a sports shop in Maltby, changing its name from Sports of Maltby to Mick Jones Sports. It benefited more people than him. When Bremner was appointed manager of Doncaster Rovers, a club with a very meagre budget, he asked Jones to supply them with equipment. 'They'd pick up the kit, I'd invoice Donny and then wait for about six months for my money,' he jokes.

Later he gravitated towards the markets in Mansfield, raising money while his son was between jobs. 'We didn't make much but it was a bit of fun, apart from the horrible winters. I wasn't bothered about my name or my reputation. I needed work so I went on the markets. It had to be done.' Only when corporate gigs at Leeds and Sheffield United were thrown his way did football reel Jones back in.

The bright lights of Leeds gave him his memories but Jones returned to his roots and retired to Anston, a village made famous by the quarries which supplied limestone for the building of the Houses of Parliament. As the years passed he was reconciled with a sport which had turfed him out prematurely. Jones never craved recognition but those who knew him best still wonder at the fact that his England career stretched to just three caps; three caps in which Jones found ample satisfaction. 'Someone once said to me, "Once you've got England on your record it never goes away. It never disappears." That's absolutely right. It's not Mick Jones, Sheffield United and Leeds United. It's Sheffield United and England. Leeds United and England. It's always there now and I love the fact it's always there.' That, to Jones, was what £100,000 felt like.

3

Brian Deane saw most things at Leeds. In the same Leeds City Boys team as David Batty, he initially did not make it at Elland Road, but not many kids from Chapeltown did in those days – the *Shoot!* magazine headline when he finally joined Leeds for a record fee: 'Ebony in Ivory'. It took Howard Wilkinson to play a 6 foot 3 inch striker on the wing, but that got Leeds into Europe via Deane's greatest goal, running the length of the pitch at Spurs. His first four years at Leeds encompassed most things: UEFA Cup, League Cup final, playing with everyone – Yeboah, Wallace, Rush, McAllister, Speed, Radebe. Then he returned to Leeds in even more turbulent times in 2004 and scored four in one match. Quiet and intriguingly emotional off the pitch, this is an illuminating insight into how hard it was for him to make it.

BRIAN DEANE: THE HARD WAY

BY DANIEL CHAPMAN

One day in Leeds in 1984, when Brian Deane was 16, he was lying on the backseat of his brother-in-law's Daihatsu, thinking what he was always thinking: he was going to be a professional footballer.

The pain in his leg didn't matter. A tackle in a match on Chapeltown Rec had just broken his tibia and fibula and dislocated his ankle, but that was secondary. He could still hear what the older lads on the sidelines had been shouting during the match: 'Five pounds if you break Deano's leg! Ten pounds if you break Deano's leg!'

They could stay on the sidelines. Brian Deane was going to be a professional footballer.

'I never forget looking back at all those people who had got their wish,' says Deane. 'And thinking, you are not going to beat me. This isn't it for me. I can't let this happen. I don't know what I was hanging onto, but I just felt there was somebody, something guiding me. A lot of things about me have been about proving people wrong.'

1984 was a great time for teenagers in Leeds who wanted to be professional footballers. John Sheridan, Scott Sellars, Tommy Wright and Denis Irwin were all playing in Eddie Gray's young Leeds United team at Elland Road; kids like Peter Swan and David Batty were getting apprenticeships. Deane knew them all, from local matches, junior trials or, in Batty's case, from school.

'Me and Batts went to Allerton Grange. We used to go past his house up in Chapel Allerton on the way to school and back; he had a lovely family, they were such nice people. At school Dave was always a bit quiet, but he was mentally strong, he would tell people what he thought. I used to see him on his own a lot, but he didn't give a shit.'

Deane's house in Chapeltown was a short walk from Batty's, and a bus ride from Elland Road, but in some ways in a different world. Deane's parents came from the Caribbean as part of the Windrush generation, invited to Britain to help build a country, but given a welcome as cold as the weather: 'They had so many issues in Leeds. There were problems getting somewhere to stay; you know the stories about "no blacks, no Irish, no dogs". There was graffiti: "Niggers Go Home." They had to work two jobs. We felt like Chapeltown was where we belonged and where we were safe. It was comforting that everybody knew each other. I've nothing but fond memories of growing up there. It was a great place, really, but it wasn't a very big area. There was a lot of racial tension in Leeds at that time and certainly Elland Road was a no-go area – we'd heard horror stories about the National Front, who had a big presence in the city, and it was frightening. As a kid I didn't really understand a lot of the things that were going on at the time, it just meant my boundaries were inside those five square miles.'

Chapeltown had everything a football-obsessed kid needed to dream: a television – to watch Argentina at the 1978 World Cup; Laurie Cunningham and Cyrille Regis playing for West Bromwich Albion; the Arsenal team that was in the FA Cup final every year – and the recreation ground, where Deane could pretend to be Regis, Alan Sunderland and Frank Stapleton. 'It was all I needed at the time,' says Deane, 'and what I felt comfortable doing.'

But it didn't have a professional football team. By 1984 Arsenal's team was changing: Viv Anderson, the first black player to play for England, was in defence, and youngsters like Chris Whyte and Paul Davis were breaking through at their local First Division club. Brian Deane's nearest team, and his target if he wanted to be a footballer, was Leeds United, but that felt far away on the other side of a frightening city. Since Terry Connor had been sold in 1983, there were no role models there for Deane, and no comfort.

'I knew Terry because he grew up in Chapeltown as well, so there was that link,' says Deane. 'But it just seemed impossible to follow him. As a community we never really imagined that we were good enough. There was some real talent there, but there was a lack of encouragement that killed a lot of people's aspirations and dreams.

'I took a bit of a leaf from Terry's book, because he had gone to Foxwood School, and looked for opportunities to get outside of the community. My desire to be a pro was so strong that I decided I wasn't going to be affected by racism, but I was scared, all the same. When I was getting the bus to go to John Smeaton School for trials with Yorkshire Amateurs, me and my friend Michael Phillips were the only two black kids out of 150, and we were genuinely scared of being beaten up.

'My friend Jeff Clarke got an apprenticeship at Elland Road, but I just never felt 100 per cent comfortable. I went down there for trials and I never forget seeing some of the pros down there, and they weren't very friendly. But I haven't forgotten that once when I went down for treatment, Paul Hart came into the physio room and he was really nice to me. He asked what I'd done, and he said he liked my shoes. He won't remember, but not a lot of people made that effort, and I will never forget that. Young kids don't forget if somebody treats them kindly – or not very kindly.'

It wasn't just Elland Road; rejection was everywhere in Leeds in the mid-1980s. Deane had a job interview at an advertising agency that turned out to be a set-up; someone sending the boss a black applicant as a joke.

'The sad thing is that people don't realise when they're doing these things that they're denying somebody an opportunity to blossom. You are crushing people's dreams. People don't understand what it's like, that you can't just brush it off, because it affects you in every single way. Try thinking about something that will make you feel vulnerable, and then imagine people encouraging that happening. How could you feel you are going to get a fair chance? People don't really understand racism. Unless they could be black for a day and go through some of the things people like me went through. They don't understand why you say you had to be better than everybody else, because it was like a boxing match where you have to knock somebody out to get a draw. That's the way you had to be to even get a chance.'

Deane would not stop working for his chance. That's what led him to Yorkshire Amateurs, aged 16, still trying to make it as a professional, playing on Chapeltown Rec against the local team, Mandela, and against the downside of living in a tight community.

'I think some of the community felt I was a sell-out for playing for Leeds City Boys, and for Yorkshire Amateurs, when all I was trying to do was get on. Some of the people on the sidelines were really saying things like, "Five pounds if you break Deano's leg! Ten pounds if you break Deano's leg!" That incident really changed things for me.'

They might have kept their money because the tackle that did break Deano's leg wasn't malicious – he was through on goal and brought down from behind, pretty much the only way to stop him. It did stop him, for eight months of painful rehabilitation, but it started something, too.

'I had to get a piggy-back into my brother-in-law's Daihatsu,' says Deane. 'I never forget, as he drove me to hospital, looking back at all those people who got their wish, and thinking, "You are not going to beat me."'

Persistence paid off at Doncaster Rovers. Leeds United's chief scout, Dave Blakey, moved there to work with the manager, Billy Bremner. Deane was fit again and writing to every club he could think of for a trial; Blakey remembered him, and invited him down. Blakey and Bremner soon left for Leeds themselves, but new manager Dave Cusack liked Deane and gave him the things he wanted: a professional contract, games and goals. It was the Third Division and in Deane's third season Rovers were relegated, but he scored a quarter of their 40 goals, taking over as top scorer from Neil Redfearn. Sheffield United had just been relegated from the Second Division, and needed a goalscorer: Deane had proven he could do it.

From 1988 until 1993 Deane proved it again and again, at higher and higher levels. His partnership with Tony Agana was the stuff dreams are made of – 'almost telepathic' says Deane. He was right-footed, Agana left-footed. When one dropped short, the other went long. When one went in the box, the other went wide. They were both fast; Deane would flick on balls for Agana, or Agana would flick them on for Deane. Dave 'Harry' Bassett was the manager, but he didn't coach them; it wasn't until Brian Marwood signed from Arsenal in 1990 that anyone talked to Deane about the space between centre-backs and full-backs. Until then it was pure instinct, hard work, football intelligence, and goals; in 1988–89 Sheffield United were promoted to Division Two, and in 1989–90 to Division

One, finishing second on goal difference behind champions Leeds.

Leeds' 4-0 win at Elland Road in April – the famous 'Go on Gary Speed' game – was vital. 'I desperately wanted to win that game,' says Deane. 'Sometimes you look at your opponent and you think you've got this one in the bag. You just need the service. And that was one game where I felt we bottled it. We lost 4-0 at Leeds and 5-0 at West Ham that season, and only lost the championship on goal difference.

'Nobody really fancied us; Leeds had players like Gordon Strachan and we were just a team that had been put together. *Calendar* and *Look North* all wanted Leeds to go up. Leeds got all the coverage and we never seemed to get any. I was disappointed that day because I turned up and I really felt like I came for business. I was open for business and ready to do some damage – but we got smashed.'

Deane's goals helped Sheffield United survive in the First Division, and he was facing Leeds again in April 1992, in very different circumstances – Leeds United's title decider.

'I was in and around Leeds and in many ways I thought, "You know what? It would be great for the city." They'd done exceptionally well. But I'm a professional and I just wanted to win, I wanted to score. But that was a crazy game, with some crazy outcomes. Leeds had some big players that day, like Strachan, Rod Wallace, Gary McAllister – big, big characters, obviously feeding on the fact they'd got to the end of the season and were in with a shout of winning the title.

'The crowd was unbelievable, on both sides. You just don't get games with crowds like that now. Those days were unbelievable, and with fans passing those stories down to the next generation, they must be thinking, "Wow, when are we going to get some of that?" We didn't have anything to lose, we just wanted to win. It was a freebie for us.'

Although it had required a detour to South Yorkshire to fulfil his ambition, it seemed inevitable that Deane would one day become a Leeds player. Tony Agana actually got there first, signing on loan in the title season after Lee Chapman broke his wrist, but then partnering him in a match against Aston Villa, when Eric Cantona dropped to the bench. But in summer 1993 Cantona was long gone and Chapman was leaving too, meaning there was a vacancy at number nine that Deane filled for £2.7 million, the most Leeds had ever spent on a player.

Elland Road had changed: the new East Stand was opening, with the largest family stand in the country; community officer Ces Podd had worked tirelessly since 1988, joining Leeds in the same month as Howard Wilkinson, to build links across the city and into the community where Deane grew up. His family and friends could watch him now, and with players like Chris Fairclough, Chris Whyte, Rod Wallace and David Rocastle, Leeds United was not a no-go area. It was all go.

The pre-season photographs in United's new ASICS kit just confirmed the feeling that this was right; Deane looking sharp in the crisp white home shirt, with a blue and yellow hoop, reunited with schoolmate David Batty, wearing blue and gold stripes. They were both holding pistols, but that was the photographer's prerogative, unless he knew something about the atmosphere behind the scenes of a club that had just tried to defend the league title but finished 17th.

'If I'm totally honest there was a little bit of an edge,' says Deane about the squad he walked into. 'There was a bit of mistrust about what had happened. I think there were players who had come in, like Steve Hodge, David Rocastle, one or two others, who thought they weren't really getting the chance they should. David Rocastle was someone I looked at and wanted to emulate, even though he was only a year older than me. I looked at him as a senior player because of his experiences and where he had been. I had a really tight relationship with Rocky, and Rod Wallace and Chris Fairclough, but it was difficult because I had decent relationships with everybody, and there was a feeling not everybody was getting a fair crack of the whip. Believe me, that was one of the best squads in the league, and if there had been a better atmosphere the football could have gone on to the next level. But by finishing 5th it justified that the manager was doing a very good job, picking a team that was winning most weeks anyway.'

Howard Wilkinson was picking his big-money striker, but after a goal on the opening day, Deane wasn't scoring. There hadn't been much coaching while he was growing up at Sheffield United, and because Deane was an England international worth £2.7 million, it was assumed he didn't need any now. But Leeds didn't play like Sheffield United, and were expecting Deane to do what Lee Chapman did. That was easier said than done.

'We had four terrific players in midfield at Leeds,' says Deane. 'Speeds, Batts, Macca and Strach. That's a midfield that is very good on the ball, that wants to keep possession. What I found for the first year was that I was used like a bounce wall, with my back to goal, so I would get the ball but I would have to give it back.

'We had overlapping full-backs, Kelly and Dorigo, but I was used to getting across defenders and attacking the ball, and they would hang crosses up in the air, so I'd have to wait for it. It just wasn't my game. I didn't know the dark arts of that. I was just somebody who was 25 years old and quick – I wanted to play on the shoulder of defenders. And I was a shadow of the player I was, because that wasn't the kind of game we were playing.'

The criticism was intense. After Deane and strike partner Frank Strandli were hauled off in a Cup game against Oxford United and read the riot act by Wilkinson, Mel Sterland, his own career about to end through injury, tried to pick him up. 'Mel's a brilliant guy,' says Deane. 'I remember him putting his arm round me and saying, "Come on, Brian. This is Brian Deane. Just think about all you've done." When someone is having their own troubles but has still got time for you, it's those words of encouragement that pull you through. But then in the *Evening Post* the next day, the headline was "These Two Gave Us Nothing" and the pictures were like mug-shots of me and Frank. And I thought, "Wow. Cheers."'

Deane couldn't take four more years playing like this, and his family and friends couldn't take four more years of Deane coming home from training and suffering through the day and night, until he had to go training again. It took a summer argument with brother Tony to wake Brian up to himself.

'I went back to Leeds and I said, "OK, this is what's going to happen. You're going to get the old Brian Deane. Brian Deane is going back to what Brian Deane does best. Being forceful, being positive, scaring people." I was going to focus on what I knew. I thought, "If anyone messes with me they will find out that I am a different person to the one who came in and was trying to fit in." It was time to show everybody that I am not a man to be messed with when I'm angry.'

Deane went back to basics, back to what he'd been doing at Sheffield United, in games and in training, doing extra fitness work with specialist coach Ed Baranowski at Don Valley Stadium. It worked. 'Damn right it did,' says Deane. 'My physicality changed within six to eight weeks. I'd done it at Sheffield United, and once I started doing it again my physical form changed. A lot of the guys could see I was putting on this muscle, and it suited my frame. All of a sudden I took some stopping.'

Other players joined in. Although Wilkinson took a while to realise it, soon half his squad was doing extra fitness sessions with Baranowski; eventually, when George Graham took over as manager, David O'Leary recommended bringing him in.

'The first to come down was Rod Wallace, and he saw the benefit. Then Gary Speed started coming down; John Pemberton, who had done it with me at Sheffield United; Carlton Palmer. We were all doing "chins", pulling yourself up on this bar about nine feet in the air, and some of us were doing three sets of six – six in front; six with one arm; six with the other; six behind your neck – that's how strong we were. And it was funny, because when some of the lads coming down for the first time had their assessment – I won't mention any names – they could only do one or two. But that was the benefit – you could measure it in six weeks.'

It worked for Deane, and it worked for Leeds. Ideas about needing players to emulate Chapman or replace Gordon Strachan faded, as young players like Gary Kelly and Noel Whelan forced thoughts towards a different future in the Premier League, and with Gary McAllister and Gary Speed prompting in midfield, Leeds turned to a front three that, in 1995, took them back to Europe – capped by Deane's solo goal at Tottenham that won qualification to the UEFA Cup in a season when he was voted supporters' player of the year.

'That goal encapsulated everything I had done, but the player of the year award meant a hell of a lot. It was redemption. To decide I was going to take control of my destiny and do it my way, and come out how I did, and have the fans actually recognising that, it showed me that the job had been done. "Well done," I patted myself on the back – you have to do that sometimes.

'We were a fit team; we were very well put together, tidy. The fans were right, that team should have been challenging – we should have got right to the end. There were some good teams around at the time. Liverpool were good, obviously Arsenal and Manchester United, but we had every right to be in the shake-up. If you look at what Rod Wallace would be like now, you have to put him in the Griezmann category. You just don't get that kind of player, small and explosive, like you did then. He was a better player than he got credit for. You have to go a long way to find someone who could score a goal like his against Tottenham. Rod would be the first to tell you that he's not the most vocal of people, but I think he's one of the players that should have been revered, and taken better care of. Some of his goals – left foot, right foot – even before I came to Leeds, I'd see them. I think he was well-respected outside the club, but he's someone who didn't get the credit he deserved.'

Tony Yeboah, on the other hand, had no problems with the limelight.

'Tony Yeboah just kind of turned up one day with his agent, and we didn't know what to expect,' says Deane. 'Even in training when he first came, he looked heavy. But it was all muscle. And he could shift. I remember being on the pitch when he scored that hat-trick in Monaco, and me and Gary McAllister just looked at each other in amazement. We were saying he had to be the best centre-forward in the world at that moment. He would try to score from the kick-off, and we were just like, "Tony – whatever you want to do, you do it." It was mesmerising to be around him. It's hard to describe because all of a sudden he would just explode. That goal he scored against West Ham, how he generated the power – just incredible. When Yeboah came everything changed. Him being in the team was good for me. We had somebody scoring goals regularly, and if you're not the one scoring regularly, then it's always good that someone is. We had a situation where sometimes our midfielders didn't track back and we'd be overrun playing 4–4–2, so we went to 4–3–3 and I was playing wide on the left because essentially I was two-footed. The advantage for me was that now I was getting the ball deep and running at people, and I could get on the back post for a header, or I could cross for people with my left foot. My motto was always: when you're in those positions give your teammates the kind of service you would want. That's what I used to focus on. I was happy being the supply, chipping in with the goals. It was more about the team.'

The UEFA Cup tie with Monaco was one of the post-title highlights of the 1990s. Yeboah's hat-trick in Monte Carlo (wearing another iconic kit of blue and green stripes) was the individual story, but that game and the second leg, lost 1-0 at Elland Road, were big team performances. Monaco had Fabian Barthez, Enzo Scifo, Basile Boli, Lilian Thuram, Sylvain Legwinski, Sonny Anderson – and a young Thierry Henry came off the bench.

'It just shows how good we were,' says Deane. 'You've got World Cup winners there, and we were up there with them. When people ask who my hardest opponent was, I say Lilian Thuram, and they'll ask when I played against him. But he was man-marking me in the second game and I hardly got a kick. And I tried everything. He was a young player, pretty much unknown, but it was one of the most humbling lessons I've had.'

Leeds seemed well placed to regularly compete with clubs like Monaco, spending £4.5 million on a World Cup star of their own, part of Sweden's bronze medal team from 1994, Tomas Brolin – but 1996 was a harsh fall from 1995's promise.

'The Coca-Cola Cup final was one of my lowest points,' says Deane, and every Leeds fan who remembers losing 3-0 to Aston Villa at Wembley will nod along. 'I started to question what my role was. The week before the final we played Everton, live on TV, and I played in a weakened team. The manager came to me and said, "Listen, this is crazy. You should be one of the first names on the teamsheet. Give me a good performance and you'll be in next week."

'The Everton team was very good – the Joe Royle era with Andrei Kanchelskis. I got man of the match on telly and I scored twice in a 2-2 draw. I came in the dressing room and the manager couldn't look me in the face. And I thought, "You're not playing next week, Brian." And I just wondered what I was supposed to do. You can talk about professionalism, but I tell you now if there's anybody who would be happy at that, and be able to keep 100 per cent focused and ready as a sub, or whatever, they're a better man than me. It really upset me, and I don't mind saying it.

'I had some friends at Villa. I spoke to them afterwards and they couldn't believe it. They got the teamsheet before the game and they were doing cartwheels. It was like saying to Villa, "Here, do you want to pick the medals up before the game?" I just thought it was a travesty. I was like, "What's going on?" Because I don't know who picked that team, but it wasn't a team to win a game, simple as that.'

Howard Wilkinson, in his first Cup final at Wembley, had picked it. 'What should have been a marvellous experience, win or lose, turned into a nightmare,' he said later. Deane was on the bench.

'I wanted to be in the stands!' Deane says. 'By kick-off any frustration I'd had with the manager had dissipated because I thought, "Well, there are two sides to every story, and he's made his decision." But I was looking at Rod Wallace in the stands and thinking, "That's where I want to be." Whatever was happening on the pitch I couldn't affect it [it was 1-0 at half-time when Deane came on for Mark Ford] – whatever it was, we were done. We were not coming back from that. I didn't want to come on. I was thinking, "Why should I be part of something that I couldn't influence in the first place, like a lamb to the slaughter?" That was my selfish opinion. But at the same time, I've got feelings, like everybody else.'

Wilkinson kept his job through the following summer's takeover, but not beyond September of the new season, when new owners Caspian replaced him with George Graham.

'I tore a groin muscle in the first game of the season and was out for 12 weeks, so I watched from a distance how things unfolded with Howard Wilkinson's situation, and it wasn't very nice. I remember when he came in and said goodbye to everybody – we all felt bad. We had all seen that everything was kind of crumbling around him, and we'd all chipped in and wanted to do well for him, because whatever you say he was always trying to do the best for the club – not only for himself, but for the players as well. But it had just lost its momentum.

'When George Graham came in, he changed the culture; he was very functional and you couldn't get close to him. There was no sitting in his office sharing tactics with players. It was, "This is what I want from you, and that's it." And the football changed, because sometimes we played eight defensive players. It was tough as a striker because people were saying, "This is the lowest-scoring season," and you're thinking, "Well, Jeez!" [Graham's] first thought was to stop conceding goals and keep the club in the Premier League. He'd go round each player, telling them what their responsibilities were, then he'd tell me, "You can just do what you want in the final third."'

Deane scored his last goal at Elland Road on the last day of the season, helping to relegate one of his future clubs, Middlesbrough, although at that point he had no thoughts of leaving Leeds. But his contract was up, and things changed when he saw his new contract details in the newspapers before they'd been offered.

'I found it wholly disrespectful. I never saw any contract details for anybody else in the papers, but being a boy from Leeds, they thought they could treat me how they wanted. No, sorry. I could see there were going to be changes at the club but I wanted to stay and be part of them. But I couldn't stay under those circumstances.'

In many ways the changes at the club that season marked the end of an era: the first five years of the Premier League, and the first generation of footballers to benefit from satellite television's largesse – even if it looks like small beer in retrospect. And in Leeds, they were five years when the city shook the industrial dust out of its hair, hailed the league champions, acquired a Harvey Nichols, hosted Euro '96 games and grew the best grassroots clubbing scene in the country.

'Things are different now in football for various reasons, but we were a close bunch. We'd go out together, we'd go for a drink together; we shared everything in the changing room. It was brilliant. It's not like now, when everybody is snapping everybody on social media. We used to go into town, there were a couple of little jazz bars; we'd go to Bibis for food. There was a club called Vague; it was a gay club, and the atmosphere in there was brilliant. We liked it because you didn't get idiots going there, it was just guys and girls having a great time.

'We were just doing what guys were doing, but we knew what our responsibilities were. We never took our foot off the pedal, but we needed that release. We'd go out, have a few drinks, go home and back in for training on Monday. Simple as that. Good times, man.'

It had taken Deane a long time and a lot of hard work to get to the good times at Elland Road. In 2004, 20 years after breaking his leg, there was a coda, as Leeds United were slipping back to where they had been in 1984, and much worse.

'Chaos – that's a good way of describing it,' says Deane. It was Leeds' first season after relegation from the Premiership and the club was still in shock. Kevin Blackwell started the season with Gary Kelly and not much else, and week to week players would appear then disappear from the line-up. Deane answered the call to help.

'It was chaos but for me it didn't really matter. I didn't join the club with any expectations other than I wanted to give what I had left, or as much as I could. If I couldn't get in the team, I'd take that on the chin, because it would mean the team was in a good place. You still had people there like Gary Kelly, who hadn't really changed in the time I was away – still the same person, a great guy. Michael Duberry was there, who I knew and had played against, and at the time he was getting a lot of stick that I felt was unfair, because of the historical issues that he'd had. Kells and Dubes were inseparable – good guys who understood the club, because they had been there while everybody else left like rats from a sinking ship, and I think it's important to remember that. People don't always understand what binds a good dressing room; you need characters like that. Dubes was fully committed, and it was very sad how he got treated by some of the people who had just taken over the club at the time. Some of the stories were horrendous.'

Amid the club's dramatic descent, though, was one story to remember, to complete a story of 20 years that started in the back of a Daihatsu – what better ending could there be?

In November 2004 Brian Deane dismissed the gathering gloom over Elland Road by scoring four goals in one game against QPR.

'Sometimes I don't realise these things, but that in itself was an achievement. At the age I was, still playing in the Championship and scoring four goals in one game, I think there were only people like Teddy Sheringham who were around my age and still doing it at that level. So it was a hell of an achievement given everything that was going on. My body was getting to the point where I couldn't do some of the things I was used to doing, and I was having to rely on being more efficient and wiser about the game. But it was one of those moments when you think, "This is why you did it." It was worth coming back for that. I've still got the boots – still with the mud from those days – still got the match ball. It felt like it was everything coming together, and now this is the reward. This is the reward for the perseverance and the dedication.'

4

Fans like players who are different. **David Prutton** was one of those during his three years at Leeds, coining the moniker 'Jesus' and once peppering an interview I did with him for *The Times* with asides about David Brent, the skinny legs of the Kasier Chiefs and the merits of Bettys tea room. 'I live in Harrogate and, I tell you, the queues for Bettys go on for miles in the summer,' he said, wearing faded Beatles t-shirt and a skull-ring. 'You get a lot of bus trips with older people getting off and, occasionally, you'll come cross one who's lost, so you put them back on track.' Prutton is just as good talking about his infamous referee-shove, the Dennis Wise era and what it felt like being a Premier League ex-pat in League One.

DAVID PRUTTON: JESUS

BY PHIL HAY

The conversation with Dennis Wise was short and unequivocal.

'If you turn me down, that's it. I won't ask again.'

David Prutton knew enough about Wise to take that threat at face value. It was January 2007 and Leeds United were trying to sign Prutton on loan, desperate for help in the middle of their worst season on record. Prutton had gone cold at Southampton and needed a club which felt more like home. He had grown up in Hull, a short walk from the banks of the Humber, but in footballing terms home was Nottingham Forest, the team where he turned professional as a teenager. After some indecision on his part, a loan to the City Ground was agreed.

'I phoned Dennis and said as nicely as I could, "Thanks but no thanks. I'm going back to Forest." Dennis was Dennis. "You only get one chance with me." I'm sure he meant it.'

Wise probably did, but neither he nor Prutton had anticipated the mayhem of the summer ahead of them, and when it arrived Leeds United's manager swallowed his pride. In finally joining the club Prutton was moved to Elland Road at the third time of asking. Leeds had first agreed terms to sign him from Southampton before the start of the 2006–07 season but Prutton was playing with an ankle injury, running off the pain each day in training, and he failed a medical. United's physiotherapist Dave Hancock – a talent in his field who was later poached by Chelsea and then the New York Knicks – told the club's manager, Kevin Blackwell, not to sign him and advised Prutton to have surgery immediately. 'Blackie got me into his office and said, "Unfortunately, it's bad news,"' Prutton says. 'I thought it would be the classic "it's bad news – you've signed" joke, but sadly it wasn't. I went back to Southampton with my tail between my legs and had the operation.'

Blackwell was dismissed within a matter of weeks and when Wise, the incendiary coach chosen by chairman Ken Bates to replace him, called Prutton in the next transfer window, it was Prutton's decision to decline. 'He'd been very adamant about me signing. He's that sort of personality, someone who expected you to say yes. I didn't think he'd call again.'

The close season in 2007, though, was a tense and uncertain one, for Leeds and for Prutton. The midfielder, at the maturing age of 26, was out of contract for the first time in his career and had no viable offers on the table after his release by Southampton. Forest, with Prutton on loan, had reached the League One play-offs, but he was sent off at a delicate stage of their semi-final defeat to Yeovil Town, shown two yellow cards for 'smashing Nathan Jones twice'. In a historical mismatch, Yeovil won 5-4 on aggregate as Forest struggled through extra-time with ten men. At full-time there was no Wembley final and no prospect of promotion. Forest, despite Prutton's old affiliation with them, let him go.

A few weeks earlier Leeds had joined Forest in League One by finishing bottom of the Championship. To crown the most destructive of years, they were declared insolvent 24 hours before the season ended and promptly bought back by Bates in a hurried takeover deal which frustrated many of the club's creditors and raised eyebrows at the Football League. By early

August Leeds had been punished with a 15-point deduction, applied to their forthcoming League One season owing to a breach of the league's rules on insolvency. Bates appealed but lost and would lose a longer arbitration battle nine months later. On 9 August, two days before Leeds' first game away at Tranmere Rovers, Wise was informed that the penalty would stand. 'Not only have they [the Football League] taken my arms and legs off, now they've cut my balls off as well,' he said. Leeds liked his tone so much that t-shirts bearing those words were sold in the club shop.

As chaos reigned and a transfer embargo ruined the start of the summer window, Wise relented and asked Prutton to come and train at Thorp Arch. It was all Leeds could do: court out-of-contract players and rely on patience and goodwill until the landscape improved. Times had changed and Wise and Prutton needed each other. 'I was fortunate in the fact that the club had gone down and had big money worries,' Prutton says. 'They were shedding high earners and cutting back too, so it opened up a window of opportunity for players like me to join, even though they couldn't actually sign me at first. The Premier League's rules meant I got double pay in my final month at Southampton, so financially there was no real stress but it was new for me. As far as other offers went, there was nothing out there.

'When we spoke I reminded Dennis that he'd told me to sod off. I was joking and he laughed it off. That situation was very black and white with him, which is how I'd describe him as a manager and a bloke. He wanted lads he could trust; lads he wouldn't find himself farting around with to keep in line. It was scattergun recruitment because it couldn't be anything else, and Christ knows how it worked, but the chemistry was just perfect. As much as we were a bunch of waifs and strays, we were all very determined to play for the club. That was apparent.'

Most of those players, Prutton included, had trained with Leeds throughout pre-season and completed a three-match tour of Germany and the Czech Republic without contracts to their names. The club's transfer embargo reduced Prutton, a former England under-21 international who Forest had sold to Southampton for a seven-figure sum five years earlier, to the level of triallist at the most dysfunctional club around.

But Thorp Arch, the complex near Wetherby where Leeds have trained for almost 20 years, is a wide, green expanse in the plush Yorkshire countryside, and Elland Road remained as 'fuck you' and intimidating a stadium as Prutton remembered: 'You couldn't get away from the fact that it was Leeds. It wasn't Leeds as people knew them but it wasn't like we were being asked to go to the arse-end of League Two either. None of us really followed what was going on above our heads, but I trusted what I was being told and what Dennis was promising me. There were always going to be contracts because, let's face it, at the back of your mind you knew that Leeds were too big to disappear, however bad it all got. I always thought it would be all right, which might just be the optimist in me. So in answer to the question "do you want to come?" it was, "Yes, let's get cracking."'

Prutton had briefly been a teammate of Wise's at Southampton, where the latter was seeing out a stellar playing career and the former was trying to make the most of his. Southampton, in 2003, was a marquee move for Prutton, the sort of transfer which many at Forest anticipated as his development hastened and his England youth career ticked over. A fee of £2.5 million was not inconsiderable by the standards of the time. For Prutton, the change of scene generated excitement and tension in equal measure – a world away from the familiarity of Nottingham and their academy. He had being schooled at Forest by Paul Hart, the retired defender who found his niche in academy coaching and took credit for Leeds twice winning the FA Youth Cup in the 1990s.

'Harty terrified the life out of us but, in the same breath, he loved you to bits too,' Prutton says. 'There was a tough-love element to the academy there: brutal at times, but only in the way that football is. It made sense to me. If you can't take a bawling out from the manager in front of your peers, especially when you deserve it, how are you going to cope with 20,000 people caning you or the local paper battering you on Monday morning? Or these days, social media? Those seeds had to be sown.

'But Southampton was a huge chance. It's what you spent your time and effort aiming for. I was part of the furniture at Forest, and it was very comfortable, but ambition takes hold. You take the move. When I got there, as a 21-year-old, there was an element of the ridiculous about it, like Forrest Gump when he's cropping up in the background of ridiculous situations with famous people. I'd be stood in the tunnel and look around to see that famous Arsenal team next to me: Henry, Vieira, Petit. Even training with players you'd only vaguely heard of who made you think, "Christ, they're miles better than I am." Some of them would push your buttons in training to see how you'd react. It was their way of finding out what kind of person you were. It was on another level, and it blew your mind a little bit. I found that every day mattered, in an obsessive way. I got into the habit of double checking where we were for training, double checking what time we were supposed to be in, double checking what we'd been told to wear for the coach. It kept you on your toes and I took it all very seriously. To look back now it's funny, as young men, what seems to be so unbelievably important.'

Prutton's career at St Mary's was defined by one incident, which still follows him around today. In the final minute of the first half of a 1-1 draw with Arsenal, on 26 February 2005, he was sent off for a foul on Arsenal's French winger, Robert Pirès. Prutton remonstrated with a linesman and then pushed referee Alan Wiley, reprising the confrontation between Paolo Di Canio and Paul Alcock at Hillsborough in 1998. Arsenal had been the opposition again when Di Canio, then with Sheffield Wednesday, barged Alcock to the floor after being shown a red card. Di Canio was banned for 11 games; Prutton was banned for ten – a 'hefty' suspension as he calls it.

'For a while I felt like I was apologising to everyone,' he says. 'The papers went to town on me and I'm clever enough to know that you're fair game when you do something like that. It rears its head every now and again. When Man City won the league, Agüero scoring in the last minute, Joey Barton went bonkers and got sent off. My lad was tiny at the time and I was sat feeding him his bottle when this feature came up on Sky Sports: "the top ten nutters", or something like that. Straightaway I knew where it was going, and, sure enough . . . It was a stupid, stupid moment and I carried it about for a long time. You could sense people wondering what I'd do next, and they were right to question me, but the criticism was way out of proportion. I was an idiot and I take ownership of the fact that I was an idiot, but fundamentally it's a football match. "Footballer acts like an idiot." It's not the world's most shocking headline. I realise that now and I can smile about it.'

Wiley let the incident go without any personal retribution. When he and Prutton next crossed paths, during the second leg of a League One play-off semi-final at the end of Prutton's first season at Elland Road, Wiley asked to keep his shirt at full-time. 'I don't know whether he felt it was something he needed to do after what had gone on, but he was more than welcome to it. We got on fine and we still do.'

The thought that Prutton might be a liability or a loose cannon did not bother Wise at all. By the opening weekend of the 2007–08 season, players like Prutton had given Wise a stronger hand than a shambolic summer should have done. Alan Thompson, whose nous and sweet left foot compensated for legs which were giving up, chose to stay on after a prior loan from Celtic. Andrew Hughes, the most obsessionally professional footballer most of his teammates had encountered, accepted an offer to join from Norwich City on the day that Leeds' 15-point deduction was confirmed. Frazer Richardson, Jonathan Douglas and Tore André Flo were left over from the squad relegated from the Championship. Robbie Blake, David Healy and Richard Cresswell cut and ran but the squad did not compare unfavourably to others in League One. Up front Wise stuck his neck out and gambled on two strikers, Jermaine Beckford and Trésor Kandol, who had previously been figures of fun at Elland Road, not that anyone had much to laugh about.

Kandol's 89th-minute winner on the first day at Tranmere immediately cut the club's negative points total from 15 to 12. He scored five goals in the first two months of the season and Beckford scored six as Leeds won seven league games back to back. Sourced from Barnet and Wealdstone respectively, the pair dovetailed perfectly.

'Wise spoke to me about Becks in pre-season and properly backed him to the hilt,' Prutton says. 'With the greatest of respect, he'd come from Wealdstone and I didn't know who he was. All I saw was this striker walking around Thorp Arch looking very comfortable in his skin. Dennis said, "Don't worry, this fella will score goals." I raised my eyebrows because

I had my doubts. It's an easy thing to say. But he was absolutely superb. He hit the ground running and never stopped.'

Kandol's influence dipped before long but Beckford's goalscoring was relentless, ending with the strike in 2010 which finally forced promotion to the Championship after three hard years in League One. A free transfer to Everton and the Premier League followed. 'Becks was ambitious and he was highly strung in the best possible sense,' Prutton says. 'If he didn't score he always got the hump. I loved that.'

Wise was a highly strung character himself: sharp, abrasive and viciously competitive, as he had been as a midfielder. The story went that when Ken Bates signed him at Chelsea in 1990, he looked Wise up and down at their first meeting and joked, "Is that all I get for £1.6 million?" Wise tapped his heart with a fist and replied, "Yeah, but I've got a big one of these."

At Leeds Prutton saw Wise as the yin to the yang of his assistant, the personable Uruguayan Gus Poyet. Poyet's charisma was absolute – a warm and flamboyant character whom the players respected. He and Wise were not so much a good-cop, bad-cop routine as a contrast in personalities which struck the right balance. 'There was a warmth between them and shades of dark and light which complemented each other perfectly,' Prutton says. 'Gus had that Latino spirit which elevated the atmosphere. Dennis was more serious but I found him funny in his own way. I liked him, no matter his reputation. People have a view of him and maybe he's misunderstood, but I always think that, deep down, people who are misunderstood don't really care what other people think of them. I mean, Dennis didn't give a fuck about that. He was very sure of himself, which went without saying because I don't think it would be going too far to suggest that there were fans at Leeds who hated him.'

That air of dissent owed itself to several factors. Even allowing for Wise's niggly reputation, he had connections with Chelsea – a black mark at Elland Road – and connections with Bates, the godfather of one of his children. After dismissing Blackwell, Bates entrusted Wise with most of the 2006–07 season, but Wise took Leeds down, into England's third tier for the first time since the club's formation in 1919. The public calls for the pair to quit were endless. Bates, with typical belligerence, ploughed on as chairman. Wise was so intent on remaining as manager that he agreed to cut his £400,000 salary in half.

By the autumn of 2007 the mood had changed. Leeds shot up the League One table, wiping out their 15-point deficit in a flash, and were unbeaten by late October. 'It was one of those situations where the squad were mirroring everything the manager wanted,' Prutton says. 'We gave Dennis that intensity and vigour, hitting him right back with everything he was giving us. It was the perfect storm where everything and everyone aligned. Then there were the crowds. We were travelling to away grounds where half or two thirds of them were filled with Leeds. You turned up and thought, "Batten down the hatches, the fucking army's here!" It was inspirational in a way that wasn't just a cliché. We were a proper football club in the broadest sense. "This is what it means and this is how we go about it." The energy was unreal.'

Then, at the end of October, Poyet left. Juande Ramos, the former Sevilla coach, had secured the manager's job at Tottenham Hotspur and asked Poyet to go with him as his number two, a year to the day after Poyet and Wise took over at Leeds. Bates, to his displeasure, learned of Poyet's impending exit on Sky Sports as he watched a televised UEFA Cup tie between Spurs and Getafe. Wise was blindsided too and powerless to stop his right-hand man leaving.

'When Gus went, the way Dennis came across changed slightly,' Prutton says. 'It's hard to explain but the dressing room and the atmosphere wasn't the same. There was a bit of a void. Dave Bassett came in as his assistant and Dave's a great guy, someone I knew, but you couldn't find a like-for-like swap for Gus. There was no one quite like him.' Poyet's defection and a gradual turn in results over Christmas raised the question of whether he had been the brains to Wise's brawn, or the real driving force. 'It's too simplistic to say that,' Prutton says. 'They were definitely a partnership. Wise had that steely resolve which brought out good things in Gus, and Gus' effervescence brought out good things in Dennis. The sum of the parts was greater than they were individually, I think. But when Gus went, it felt like a matter of time until Dennis went too.'

For Wise, the crunch came at the end of January. A Londoner at heart, he refused to move his family north and was commuting from the capital as much as he could. In spite of that, he went days at a time without seeing them. The sense that he and his players might be feeling the pace of the season, underlined by a dip in form, was vindicated when Wise resigned suddenly after a 1-1 draw with Luton Town on 26 January 2008. An injury-time equaliser at Kenilworth Road left him looking exhausted. On the quiet, Newcastle had offered him a director of football role, highly paid and free from the stress of travelling all over the country. Wise considered his options and quit.

'It became the most ridiculous weekend,' Prutton says. 'We'd stayed down south after the Luton game because we were playing at Southend on the Tuesday night. Dennis had gone, that much we knew, and Dave Bassett took a quick, almost pointless, training session on the Tuesday morning after which he got onto the coach, shook our hands and told us he was going too. We were sat there, looking at each other and thinking, "So who the fuck is taking the team tonight?" There was no one left.' Gwyn Williams, a long-time ally of Bates' and Leeds' technical director, did the honours without distinction, sitting quietly in the dugout as Leeds lost 1-0.

'Gwyn's skillset didn't really include coaching, let's say that,' Prutton says. 'He did what he could but the whole world should have backed us to lose that night.'

Leeds, despite the confusion, already had their replacement in the form of Gary McAllister, the club's old midfielder and title winner who had flown to Bates' apartment in Monte Carlo to finalise his contract the previous day. McAllister picked up the pieces of a season which still had potential but required a shot in the arm. After a slow first month, he delivered impressively with a streak of seven wins in nine games. The loan signing of Dougie Freedman from Crystal Palace in March was perfectly timed.

Freedman's goals won the crowd but Prutton had himself become a focal point, nicknamed 'Jesus' by Leeds' support on account of his long hair and biblical beard. His performances in that season were light on goals, in keeping with his career, but his influence was keen, and the *Yorkshire Evening Post* player of the year award went to him by a large margin. It was often said that in a year when Leeds sought divine inspiration, the son of God was the right signing at the right time.

'Growing my hair was something I'd wanted to do when I was a kid but my school didn't allow it,' Prutton says. 'Then I was in a youth team that didn't allow it because of how Paul Hart was and how he ran things at Forest. You get to the age where you're old enough to make your own decisions, so I grew it long and the "Jesus" thing took on a life of its own. The Leeds fans loved it and it was the thing opposition fans jumped on instantly, but I'd always seen abuse like that as character-building. I found the whole thing very amusing.'

Throughout the latter stages of that term, Leeds and Carlisle United were side by side in the play-off positions. Swansea City took the title and Forest avoided more trauma by finishing second and earning automatic promotion. The play-off semi-finals paired Leeds and Carlisle together, inspiring an engrossing fight in which Leeds squeezed through to Wembley by the smallest of margins. Freedman buried a priceless goal in the 96th minute of the first leg at Elland Road, restricting a fluent Carlisle side to a 2-1 win.

'That changed everything,' Prutton says. 'Suddenly we were right back in it when, really, we'd been in big trouble. The confidence was there and it wouldn't have been there at 2-0.'

In the second leg at Brunton Park, Jonny Howson, Leeds' academy-grown midfielder, came of age with two goals, the latter driven in from 18 yards in the last seconds of normal time. The celebrations at the final whistle were unrestrained.

'I've got a photo somewhere – and I never kept much of that stuff – of me and Casper [Ankergren, Leeds' goalkeeper] on the pitch at the end,' says Prutton. 'You can see the raw emotion and you can see that everyone is absolutely buzzing. The adrenaline's flowing and to look at it, you'd think we'd been promoted. You can feel that sense of not believing you've done it, even though there's still a game to go. Maybe that crept into the final. Maybe we peaked too soon.'

Ten days later Leeds were beaten in the final at Wembley by Doncaster Rovers, losing to a header from James Hayter in the second half. McAllister had prepared in the manner of a Premier League manager, taking his squad to the seclusion of Champneys in Hertfordshire and spending the night before the game in London's five-star Landmark Hotel, but Wembley was one game too far – their 55th of a season which burned in 90 minutes. 'Wembley's a funny place,' Prutton says. 'The pitch is huge, the stadium's cavernous and on the occasions when I've worked there since, the whole atmosphere can make you leggy. "Heavy-legged" is how I'd describe our performance that day. There was a lethargy to that performance which belied the energy we attacked the season with. It was the worst time for us to play like that and the better team won. It hurt. Mickey Walker was on the staff at Doncaster and I got chatting to him afterwards. As he said, "The play-off final's a great day out – but only if you win."'

It would prove McAllister's only chance. Leeds made good ground at the start of the 2008–09 season, but the Scot lost control of it before Christmas. Beckford tore a hamstring, the club were beaten on a swamp of a pitch by Histon in the FA Cup's second round, and four straight league defeats put McAllister against a wall. Leeds sacked him after a 3-1 loss at MK Dons on 20 December. Bates, who rarely attended away fixtures, had taken in that game as a guest of MK Dons manager and former Chelsea midfielder Roberto Di Matteo. He summoned McAllister to Elland Road the following morning.

For some in the dressing room the dismissal was a relief. 'I had no problem with Gary,' Prutton says. 'He'd extended my contract, which wasn't the only reason I liked him, and he gave me a fair crack of the whip. But that decision showed the *Sliding Doors* aspect of football. Hughesy [Andrew Hughes] was as good as out the door under Gary. He then became a big part of what happened under Simon Grayson. Likewise Bradley Johnson, who was miles away on loan at Brighton. I don't think Gary lost the dressing room, but enough players were disenchanted with results for the dressing room to be affected. When you set high standards in your first season – the football we played in the build-up to the play-off final was cracking stuff – and then fail to match them in your second, fingers start to get pointed.'

Grayson was another Leeds old boy, with a smaller reputation than McAllister's but the added kudos of having won promotion from League One as manager of Blackpool. It did not take long for his ability at that level to show itself. Leeds, despite the decline under McAllister, made the play-offs before losing to Millwall in the semi-finals. The following year, in 2010, the club scrambled over the line and claimed automatic promotion after surviving a horrible loss of nerve around Easter. An additional feather in Grayson's cap came from an FA Cup third-round win over Manchester United, humiliation on a scale which Sir Alex Ferguson had not experienced at Old Trafford.

Prutton, increasingly, watched from a distance, growing more and more peripheral. The change of manager worked for Hughes and Johnson but did not do much for him. 'I found myself getting very detached,' Prutton says. 'I wasn't playing enough and it was purgatorial because I had no idea if or when I'd get back in. Simon's not a confrontational guy and, anyway, the results were good. If I went and banged his door in, why would he change the team? I got that. Robert Snodgrass was a more talented player than me. Jonny [Howson] went on to play in the Premier League, and so did Bradley. I always felt Neil Kilkenny was a very good player and, ultimately, the team were going places. I had a manager who didn't like an argument, and I knew that if I went into his office and started having a go the scenario would have been ridiculous. I think all I wanted was to feel like people knew I was still there. First you're on the pitch then you end up being on the bench. Then you're travelling to games but you're not getting stripped. Then you're not even travelling. Personally, the situation began to grate and when I came to leave and asked Simon about it, he ummed and aahhed. But in the years since, I've found him very good company. That's the ironic thing. It was like getting to know him back to front: as a boss first, and then as a bloke.'

A demoralised Prutton found his approach to training crossing the boundaries of reasonable force. 'When Michael Doyle joined from Coventry I could tell in his first training session that he was going straight into the team, so in one tackle I left a bit on him,' Prutton says. 'He turned round and called me a dickhead, which no doubt I was. We'd laugh about it now, but that's what it does to you.'

The frustration was contrary to Prutton's personality and wit. Throughout his years at Leeds he attended regular yoga sessions in Harrogate and practised it before and after training sessions at Thorp Arch. Curious teammates began to take an interest. It was therapeutic, but in Prutton's mind it was also an antidote to football's culture of superstition, something Don Revie invented at Leeds and which Grayson, in particular, embraced. 'At first a few of the lads were a bit bemused by it but I carried on with yoga right to the end of my career. There were physical benefits, but I also felt the placebo side of knowing you were doing as much as you could to be in the best possible shape all the time. As you get older you realise that preparation is ridiculously important. The daft thing about football is that you spend the first half of your career praying to everyone, kissing things or wearing the same socks in the hope of buying a bit of good luck. Then you find out that if you do the right things, nine times out of ten it'll all work out anyway. It's the difference between being ready and crossing your fingers. Basically, the lap-of-the-Gods stuff is horseshit.'

The crunch for Prutton came in January 2010 when he left on loan for Colchester United, midway through Leeds' promotion season. He knew it was time to go when, on another match day where he had failed to make the 18, the stadium announcer at Elland Road asked him to take to the pitch at half-time and entertain the crowd. 'I'd basically had a haircut. They thought it would be a laugh to have a bit of fun about it. I'm sure the intentions were good but my first reaction was, "Fuck me, is this what it's come to? I am some sort of cheerleader or court jester now." They probably thought I'd be buzzing off that, but I was totally pissed off.'

Prior to matches at Elland Road Peter Lorimer, Leeds' record goalscorer and youngest ever player, held pre-match functions for supporters at the club's pavilion across Lowfields Road. Prutton became a regular on stage. 'Ian Miller [Grayson's assistant] would come round us lads who weren't playing and ask us to nip over to Lorimer's Bar and take some questions for ten minutes. The last time he came to me he must have seen the look on my face. He knew. There was nothing left to ask me or for me to say. I'd done it too often. The fans were bored of it and I was bored of it. After I left, it turned out that Leeds were playing Colchester at Elland Road a couple of weeks later. I was on loan so I couldn't play. I got a call from Ian saying, "I'm just checking how you are and, by the way, could you do Lorimer's Bar for us this weekend?" I was about to lose it when he starting howling down the phone.'

Prutton's move to Colchester became permanent inside a month. Sat in a hotel in Essex, in the days before gushing Instagram goodbyes, he decided to break from the convention of farewell interviews by writing an open letter and asking Leeds to publish it on their website. In it he described his time at Elland Road as 'one of the privileges of my life so far' and signed off as 'David Prutton (aka Prutts, aka Jesus)'.

'Social media hadn't really blown up then but the club asked me if I wanted to do an interview and I felt as if I'd only come out with all the old clichés and platitudes. Instead, I told them I'd write down my thoughts for them to publish if they wanted to. That letter was written in the Holiday Inn in Colchester, which struck me as a bleak place to be pouring my heart out, but I wanted to get it all down while I had the thoughts in my head and before the cynicism kicked in. I was conscious of not wanting it to be twee or attention-seeking. It was just an honest expression of the appreciation I felt. When you come out of somewhere like Leeds, you can't help wondering if it's the last time that you're going to get to play for a big club. You start to put your career in perspective. It got me thinking in a rose-tinted way: "Do you know what? I played for a club who I used to watch on TV and who, as a kid, I never thought I'd play for. A club I'd have killed to play for as a kid." In that instant, you become a schoolboy again. Playing for Leeds United. How cool is that?'

5

David Batty is a recurring theme throughout this book. He is one of the great enigmas, dismissed by outsiders as a one-dimensional footballer, when really he played in a way most of us would quite like to live. Anthony Clavane has nailed his significance here, so here are a few rudimentary stats to set the scene: 301 appearances, four goals, 42 England caps, one World cup penalty shoot-out miss, pushing 50, £11 million transfer fees, one in a million.

DAVID BATTY: BEING BATTY – THE LIFE AND TIMES OF A RECLUSIVE, ENIGMATIC, ICONOCLASTIC MAVERICK

BY ANTHONY CLAVANE

David Batty was born in 1968 in Leeds, Yorkshire, England. This was a year when all three – the city, the county and the country – were on top of the world. By the time he joined Leeds United, in 1985, as a skinny, floppy-haired 16-year-old, they had all been knocked off their perches. At the end of 1998, the year his penalty miss against Argentina ended England's hopes of reaching the World Cup quarter-finals, he returned to a new Leeds, as David O'Leary's first signing, and a new era of hope.

Batty would never say such a thing, but he managed, during his 18-year career, to put a bit of pride back into Leeds, Yorkshire, England. In his own small, modest, unflashy way he played a part in the revival of the city, the county and the country. And then he disappeared.

Being Batty, he would have no time for such overblown claims. No time for grandiose notions of Leeds, Yorkshire, England. No time for fanciful theories or big ideas. No time for any ideas at all, really, big or small. And certainly no time for nuanced analyses of tactics or meticulously worked out, over-detailed strategies – during his first spell at Leeds he famously switched off during manager Howard Wilkinson's long, ponderous, often unfathomable team talks. He didn't like meetings. He didn't like being told what to do.

'It's against all that I am,' he once said. 'I just wanted to do what I wanted, when I wanted.' Which is a very Leeds,

Yorkshire, England kind of thing to say. A very northern, working-class, maverick kind of thing. Just get on with it, don't fanny around, do what you need to do to win. Let your football do the talking. Everything else is propaganda.

And if anyone gets any ideas, especially ones above their station, bring them back down to earth – or, in the case of Sampdoria's left-back Marco Lanna, knock them over the advertising hoardings head first – with a thud.

Once, at a press conference to announce the signing of Eric Cantona, Wilkinson – another forthright, plain-speaking, no-nonsense Yorkshireman – made a good joke at Batty's expense. 'Eric gives interviews on art, philosophy and politics,' he deadpanned. 'A natural roommate for David Batty.'

Being Batty, he will probably not accept the ideas expressed in this chapter. He probably won't even read it. He probably hasn't even read his own autobiography. He's a doer not a talker or a thinker or someone who is prone to arguing that, in his own small way, he might have played a part in the revival of Leeds, Yorkshire, England.

I see him as a natural roommate both for Arthur Machin – the protagonist in David Storey's *This Sporting Life* – and the Leeds artist Damien Hirst. Storey, a miner's son who was born and brought up in Wakefield, Yorkshire, England, paid for his scholarship at London's Slade School of Fine Art in the 1950s by playing professionally for Leeds Rugby League. He was part of that extraordinary generation of socially mobile post-war novelists who wrote almost exclusively about the lives of the northern working class.

Published in 1960, and regarded as one of the best novels ever written about sport, its antihero, Machin, embodies a defiant, us-against-the-world, two-fingered Yorkshireness. At one point he sneers, 'There are no stars in this game. Just men like me.' This completely sums up Batty's outlook. As Billy

Bremner, Leeds' greatest ever player, and the manager of the club when Batty signed on as an apprentice, put it, 'Side before self every time.'

Like Hirst, Batty went to Allerton Grange School in north Leeds. In his youth, the maverick artist loved to shock – and stick it to – the establishment, once creating a frozen cast of his head from nine pints of his own blood. In Batty's very early youth, at a Scott Hall Middle School show-and-tell, he shocked the educational establishment – well, one of his teachers – by producing a couple of severed, bloody fingertips, which he explained in his autobiography had been chopped off during an accident and had been 'rotting away for about four years at the back of the wardrobe'.

In 1985, when Batty joined Leeds from Tingley Athletic, a few months after the miners called off their bitter, brutal, year-long strike to save the coal industry (and their tightly knit, working-class, industrial, mainly northern, communities) Hirst produced his first successful collage, a piece called *Expanded from Small Red Wheel*. 'I had mixed feelings,' Hirst later reflected. 'While I was creating things myself, I was also somehow cheating and getting all this stuff from Mr Barnes.'

Mr Barnes was a next-door neighbour who one day, like Batty after he retired in 2004, just disappeared. It turned out he had been re-housed by the council, but Hirst broke into his neighbour's house and came across an amazing store of objects. There was 60 years of existence: parcels of money, alarm clocks, hundreds of tubes of toothpaste, magazines and so on. The entire house was an installation, and it inspired a series of collages that caught the attention of the London art world. One critic argued that Hirst and his fellow Young British Artists, quite a few of whom hailed from Leeds, Yorkshire, England – part of an extraordinary generation of socially mobile 1990s artists – were informed by a 'sense of performative proletarian iconoclasm'.

When our reclusive, enigmatic, iconoclastic, maverick retired from football, and then effortlessly dropped off the radar, he didn't, of course, completely disappear. He left behind a legacy, an enduring persona, a personal myth. *In Books Do Furnish a Room* Anthony Powell wrote, 'It is not what happens to people that is significant, but what they think happens to them.' And, added the author, what others think of them. Everyone, Powell argued, has a personal myth. He was writing about fictional characters but the axiom can be applied equally to footballers, especially those who, like Batty, played a small part in some of the key moments of the sport's recent history.

Since retiring, 14 years ago, Batty has written an autobiography, given a couple of where-are-they-now? interviews (one to me in 2007 and another to *The City Talking* in 2015), and that's about it, really. In Dave Simpson's fine book about the 1991–92 Leeds side, *The Last Champions*, he was described as the Lord Lucan of football. There have been no stints in management, coaching or media punditry. No appearances on *A Question of Sport*, *Strictly* or *I'm a Celebrity*. This chapter is a collection of snapshots, a collage of some important episodes in the life and times of a great footballer who, without any fanfare, has removed himself from the limelight. It is my take on Batty, on Being Batty, on his life and times. It is what I think happened to him – and to Leeds, Yorkshire, England – during his first 35 years of existence.

1968

Apart from two Second Division titles, Leeds United had won nowt during their first 50 years of existence. You wait ages and then two major trophies come along at once. The drought ended in March 1968 when Don Revie's combative young side won the League Cup, beating Arsenal 1-0 at Wembley thanks to a thunderous volley from left-back Terry Cooper. Then, two months later, they won the Inter-Cities Fairs Cup, a two-legged victory over Ferencváros. Revie's great team were to finish the decade on a high; the following year they were league champions with a record 67 points.

In 1968 Leeds Rugby League, the best team of its era, triumphed in the famous 'Watersplash final', beating Wakefield Trinity thanks to an infamous last-minute penalty miss by Don Fox. Yorkshire County Cricket Club, graced by the formidable quartet of Geoffrey Boycott, Ray Illingworth, Brian Close and Freddie Trueman, were crowned county champions for the third successive season. And Alf Ramsey's England, the reigning world champions, finished third in the European Championship.

When, two years later, seven United players – Terry Cooper, Paul Reaney, Mick Jones, Norman Hunter, Paul Madeley, Allan Clarke and Jack Charlton – were called up for England's provisional World Cup squad, the 1960s' resurgence of Leeds, Yorkshire, England appeared to be complete.

More than any other Leeds player in the two excellent sides he played in at Elland Road – Howard Wilkinson's and, at the turn of the millennium, David O'Leary's – Batty embodied the spirit of Revie's legendary team. It was there in his style of play, his passion and desire, his lack of airs and graces, his full-blooded physicality, his knack of roughing up opponents. Especially the last two.

He had no time for prima donnas. Being Batty meant cutting the Flash Harries down to size, winding up the high and mighty. Like Sampdoria's Roberto Mancini, during a pre-season friendly. The self-admiring Italian – described in one adoring profile as 'a thinker, an artist . . . the pitch was his notepad' – couldn't cope with Batty's brazen, tongue-in-cheek provocations, at one point running the length of the pitch to lunge at a player who had just nudged one of his teammates, the aforementioned Lanna, over the Elland Road hoardings. The provocateur adroitly stepped out of the way and Mancini's humiliating air-tackle was greeted with ironic cheers by the Batty-adoring home crowd. The high-and-mighty, self-admiring Italian had been made to look somewhat foolish.

But, most of all, being Batty meant a total commitment to 'the Cause'. 'In the Yorkshire philosophy of sport,' the renowned cricket correspondent Jim Kilburn once explained, 'it is impossible to be too keen on winning a competitive engagement.' None of your purists' play-up-chaps-and-play-the-game guff. Batty was no gentleman amateur. His game was about strict discipline, being ultra-competitive and having a fierce will to win. And getting your retaliation in first. He was the last of a dying breed, the last Revie-ite hard man, the last of a generation to be hewn from Yorkshire's decaying industrial towns.

At other points in his career, he was involved in a punch-up with a teammate, broke another teammate's jaw in a training game and was banned for six games for pushing a referee.

According to Tony Dorigo, left-back in Wilkinson's 1992 title-winning team, 'he was a nightmare. We started mucking about, playing cards for ages, and I kept winning and winning. I tried to lose but I just kept winning. So he was getting more and more annoyed. So then he whacks me with a pillow. So I get a pillow, and I whack him with a pillow. He then got a rolled-up magazine and he's whacking me with that. Next thing he picks up a silver tray that the food comes on and just flings that across and smacks me right in the teeth. I'm thinking, "I'd better stop here, because this could get really serious!" It didn't matter what you did, he was coming back with something harder.'

These, and other such stories, could be lifted from any one of the Revie team's autobiographies. They echo Jack Charlton's threat to knock Norman 'Bite Yer Legs' Hunter's block off as a Leeds fan shouted, 'Go arn, Norman, 'ave a go at him'; Big Jack chasing a Valencia defender halfway round the pitch after the Spaniard had punched him; Bremner, described by Michael Parkinson as 'ten stone of barbed wire', hurling his shirt to the ground after scrapping with Kevin Keegan at Wembley; Hunter lamping Frannie Lee after another dive by the Derby striker; Gary Sprake decking a lad at the Mecca after being accused of eyeing up the lad's girlfriend; Les Cocker, Revie's right-hand man, telling his defenders to go in hard with the first tackle, the one the referee never books you for.

Revie's side were a team of tough, combative players, a tight-knit squad of working-class mavericks who, collectively, transcended the limitations of their individual, industrial, working-class backgrounds. They had earned their right to play by being the hardest group of players in the land. The 'Dirty Leeds' label put the fear of god into their opponents. The only time the great Georgie Best ever wore shinpads was at Elland Road. 'I hated playing against them,' said Best. 'They had a hell of a lot of skill, but they were a bloody nightmare.' Similarly no one liked playing against Batty, the son of a Leeds binman, the bloody nightmare who came to be defined by his Revie-ite, keep-fighting-till-the-end, never-accept-defeat, don't-let-the-bastards-grind-you-down edge.

1985

Like Revie's players, however, he was underestimated. Like Dirty Leeds there was far more to his game than hard work, fierce commitment, full-blooded physicality, roughing and winding up opponents. But his personal myth was that he was a 'mere' enforcer, a protector of the back four, a tireless forager. Someone whose function was to break up opposition attacks and give the ball to better players who would then launch penetrative, eye-catching attacks. At St James' Park, the ball-winning Yorkshireman was often portrayed as the odd one out in teams noted for playing – as one of his managers there once put it – 'sexy football'.

This point was ironically conveyed on a Channel 5 poster, advertising 'Ruud Gullit's sexy football', in which Batty's head was superimposed onto the image of a male model in stockings and suspenders. However, as another Newcastle manager, Kevin Keegan, observed, it was not until a coach had worked on the training ground with Batty that he could appreciate his outstanding virtues.

When Batty arrived at Elland Road in 1985 – the year of the Heysel tragedy, the Bradford fire, the Luton–Millwall riot; the year *The Times* described football as 'a slum sport played in slum stadiums and increasingly watched by slum people' – there was a tangible sinking feeling in Leeds, in Yorkshire and in England. The city seemed to be slipping into poverty and isolation and out of the mainstream of British society. The 1984 miners' strike reinforced the view that the Tories were fighting a civil war against the north, and that the police had become a brutal arm of a heartless government. The defeat of the miners marked the beginning of the end for the coal industry – and for a tight-knit collectivism that had sustained traditional industrial communities for the past 100 years. The strike was fought, and lost, mainly in Yorkshire.

Citing the 1985 football disasters at Bradford and Heysel, Prime Minister Margaret Thatcher demonised working-class football fans, like the miners, as the 'enemy within', and announced the introduction of compulsory identity cards. To Thatcher, both the coal and football industries were now lame ducks; backward-looking, reluctant to entertain change, and part of a doomed proletarian culture. They were symptoms of an embittered, run-down country, resigned to failure.

In 1985 Yorkshire's cricket team, which for the first seven decades of the twentieth century had been the gold standard of the sport – winning 26 out of 60 championships and sharing one of the others – were languishing in the wilderness, paralysed by bitter infighting, an outmoded, insular mindset and a dearth of new talent. The county's industrial towns and cities had not only been crippled by the decline of manufacturing industry but also concreted over by urban motorways, flyovers and tower blocks. As the corpses of its dead parent industries slowly rotted, Leeds became a tough and unforgiving place. And Elland Road became the home of a nasty, embittered and racist element. There was a growing aura of menace, a climate of fear and paranoia. The city, like its football club, battened down the hatches and adopted a bunker mentality. Property experts advised businesses to move out. The town centre became a night-time haunt of disorderly youths, tramps and alcoholics.

During the late 1970s and early-to-mid 1980s the city closed ranks and folded back into the worst of itself. But Batty arrived at a moment of transition. Towards the end of the eighties Leeds began to get back up on its feet, scrub itself clean and to start all over again. Its old manufacturing base was disappearing but a thriving service sector was expanding to fill the gap.

Bremner, at first, saw Batty as a lightweight. As an apprentice, the teenager stood at five foot four and weighed eight stone. So Bremner began to build up his mentee's strength. As the Scot's former boss Revie did with his own homegrown youngsters, he got Batty to drink sherry with a raw egg stirred into it every morning. 'I think he saw a lot of himself in me,' said Batty. Bremner was unable to revive his beloved club but Wilkinson, who was appointed in 1988, awoke the sleeping giant.

His first act was to remove all the pictures of Billy and the rest of the Revie team from the walls, an exorcism of sorts. But, like the Don, Wilkinson was a deep-thinking technocrat, a single-minded Yorkshireman who paid great attention to detail and left nothing to chance. In his Leeds team, like in Revie's, there was no place for vanity, selfishness or greed. His players were mercilessly well prepared and rigorously drilled. Batty, a player who embodied the grit, commitment, aggression – and skill – of the Revie years, was at the heart of this new era. With Gordon Strachan, Gary McAllister and Gary Speed, he would form the best midfield in the country.

In 1990 Leeds were promoted to the top flight as Second Division champions. Batty spent the summer helping his dad – a Leeds City Corporation binman – on his rounds. In their first year back in the First Division they finished fourth. The following season they won the league, becoming the last champions of the pre-Premier League era.

Batty's only weakness was a lack of goals. There were affectionate cries of 'shoot' from Leeds fans whenever he received the ball inside the opposing team's half. He only scored twice in his first spell at Leeds, against Manchester City and Notts County. The strike against City, in a 3-0 win at Elland Road, should have been upstaged by Dorigo's wonder goal in that game. It wasn't. 'Batty scores,' Dorigo recalls. 'Oh my God. It was like an earthquake, the noise. It was a shitty tap in. Doesn't matter, mine was forgotten.'

1998

Between Batty's penalty miss against Argentina in the France '98 World Cup and Leeds United's barnstorming Champions League run of 2001 – the year Yorkshire's cricket side, after 32 barren years, were crowned county champions – a new Leeds, a new Yorkshire, a new England came into being.

As a player who was a throwback to the Revie era, and the pounding heartbeat of Wilkinson's honest, direct, title-winning side, Batty had one foot in the old football world. As a player who, since leaving Leeds at the dawn of the all-singing-all-dancing Premier League era to star in two – as Gullit would say, sexier sides – he had the other foot in the new football world. The new England.

His 42-cap, international career spanned the decade English football 'came home'. Or at least tried to. He made his international debut in a 3-0 win against Russia in 1991, aged 22, when the domestic game was still basking in the euphoria generated by Bobby Robson's team who, the previous year, had reached the World Cup semi-finals. This was also the year the FA's document 'Blueprint for the Future of Football' argued that the sport should follow the affluent middle-class consumer. The new football's bible was Nick Hornby's *Fever Pitch*, a bestselling, touchy-feely, confessional, middle-class memoir which sold more than a million copies in the UK and launched a thousand lad lit tomes. By the time Batty made his final appearance, in a goalless draw with Poland in 1999 – he was sent off – English football had been completely rebranded, dextrously soaring into a different stratosphere.

Like Tony Blair's New Labour, elected in 1997, football had ditched its cloth cap image, become part of Cool Britannia and embraced a new world of glamour, glitz and celebrity. By the time Batty quietly slipped away from his club, county and country in 2004, the new Leeds, new Yorkshire, new England had begun to be exposed as a hallucinatory flight of fancy.

In between leaving Wilko's Wonders and joining O'Leary's babies, Batty had become a much better player. He had transcended the limitations of his functional, ball-winning, hard man background and was now recognised as a great passer of the ball, an astute midfielder who dictated play, kept possession, read the game and spread the ball; the fulcrum of a Leeds team which, he noted, 'had a different type of player' to the Wilkinson incarnation and 'was more enjoyable to play in and probably more enjoyable to watch'. However, as he also pointed out, 'We didn't win anything . . . Wilko's team was more effective, which is what it's all about. It was a winning formula.'

Winning was part of his identity as a Yorkshireman. In sport, as in society as a whole, winners prosper and losers go to the wall. 'We don't play cricket for fun,' as Wilfred Rhodes, who personified Yorkshireness during the great period of the county cricket team's domination in the early 20th century, insisted. 'We play to win.'

Batty had been a winner at both Wilkinson's Leeds and Kenny Dalglish's Blackburn. Wilkinson had sold him to Rovers in 1993, using the proceeds to rebuild a new team – Carlton Palmer, anyone? – which then came perilously close to being relegated. Being Batty, when Dalglish's side won the title he refused to collect his winners' medal, citing the restricted number of his appearances (due to injury). In 1996 he joined Keegan's high-fliers, whom he later called 'the best side I ever played in'. But Newcastle's we'll-score-one-more-than-you, all-singing-all-dancing crowd-pleasers threw the title away and he was denied a third league triumph.

Back at Leeds, the only team he was prepared to sign for despite interest from several top clubs (including Real Madrid), he was part of another superb midfield quartet – combining brilliantly with Lee Bowyer, Olivier Dacourt and Harry Kewell – and an exciting, upwardly mobile side who stormed their way into the Champions League last four, winning admirers at home and abroad. As O'Leary's side reinvented itself for the new football era, the city was transformed into a shiny, corporate entity, a boom-time, celebrity-city-living metropolis. New markets opened up and new money fuelled a post-industrial, postmodern convulsion. The city centre was, suddenly, dotted with pavement cafés, minimalist restaurants, designer-boutique hotels, cappuccino bars and chic clubs. Derelict mills, warehouses and scrapyards were converted into loft apartments, offices and hotels.

And then came the implosion. Dressing-room divides, damaging court cases, downward mobility. A byword for financial mismanagement. A textbook definition of hubris.

Failure to qualify for the Champions League for two seasons running triggered O'Leary's sacking and produced the then-largest loss by an English football club; Leeds were £79 million in debt by the time chairman Peter Ridsdale, nicknamed Father Christmas by agents for the way he would give in to their outrageous demands, resigned.

Ridsdale's extravagance was not very Leeds–Yorkshire–England. Not very Batty. Being Batty, he didn't belong in this spend-spend-spend era. His two other teams, Blackburn and Newcastle, had been run by rich local worthies and, briefly, given the Manchester United global mega-brand a run for its money. But in the age of oligarch owners like Roman Abramovich, bloated celebrities like David Beckham and an ever-swelling football economy – mind-blowing TV contracts, rocketing ticket prices, a disconnection with traditional, industrial communities – the People's Game was being transformed beyond recognition. As English football was reincarnated as a globally dominant, commercial free-for-all, a high-octane, round-the-clock, football-never-sleeps new era, players like Batty appeared to be yesterday's men.

The 1998 World Cup quarter-final against Argentina brought into sharp focus the differences between the over-hyped David Beckham and the under-appreciated David Batty. It was, in a way, a tale of two Davids. The former was initially vilified for his red card, following a petulant trip on Diego Simeone, but soon metamorphosised into a global mega-celebrity, the world's most famous footballer. If he had not been sent off, Beckham would have been one of the five penalty takers during the shoot-out – and expected to score. Instead it was left to the goal-shy Batty to step up to the plate. His spot-kick was, inevitably, saved by Carlos Roa, and the new England, boasting the likes of Beckham, Shearer, Owen and Scholes, crashed out of the World Cup. This failure to live up to expectations was a narrative which haunted the so-called Golden Generation throughout the 'noughties' and beyond. Featuring a series of world-class players – such as Lampard, Ferdinand, Rooney – whose clubs dominated Europe, this generation belonged to an age of paparazzi journalism, 'Wags' and pampered, over-exposed, ego-driven superstars.

Batty always saw himself as a character actor rather than a bill-topper. He treated football as a day job not a matter of life and death. He preferred caravanning in North Yorkshire with his wife and twins to jet-setting off to sunnier shores. He was patriotic but didn't shout it from the rooftops; when lining up before an England game for the national anthem, he would look into the TV camera and pull faces at his sons George and Jack, watching back home. Some of his former teammates claimed he didn't even like the game.

Between 1998 and 2004 English football's marketing men and women used Beckham's 'journey' – from Public Enemy Number One to the poster boy of the new England – to tell a new national story and to attract TV, sponsorship and corporate deals. Like Beckham, there was no way Batty would be defined by 1998. But he didn't use the game to redeem and reinvent himself. As in the Kipling poem, he treated those 'two impostors', triumph and disaster, 'just the same'. The calm, almost anticlimactic way he celebrated Leeds' title win in 1992, keeping hold of his cup of tea live on television whilst sitting on Lee Chapman's sofa, provides a wonderful vignette of the former. And, six years later in France, there would be no theatrics, no Gazza-esque tears, no Pizza Hut adverts. 'I can't explain why, but I have never dwelt on a bad result,' he explained.

Batty's last season in football was Leeds United's last in the top flight. After O'Leary was sacked Batty was frozen out by the new coach, Terry Venables, recalled by El Tel's replacement Peter Reid and then ostracised by Eddie Gray. It wasn't a great way to end a distinguished 18-year career. In May 2004 his hometown club dropped out of the Premiership. They have remained in the wilderness ever since. Being Batty he, too, disappeared, washing his hands of the game and retiring to obscurity. 'He is all but forgotten now,' wrote the sportswriter James Oddy. 'Leeds fans will always retain a certain soft spot for him, but on a wider level, he is rarely, if ever, mentioned. He never appears as a pundit, or pens a ghostwritten article in the press. He hasn't had a go at management or coaching. He wrote an autobiography, but oddly for someone in the public eye that has served as his only real statements on his career and what he witnessed.'

6

Those new to football may pretend this is not a rivalry, but when these two teams do play the atmosphere is like no other. Lee Sharpe once said Sir Alex Ferguson's pre-match talk was: 'Get in there, get a result and get out as quickly as we can because we are not welcome here.' The enmity has crossed the line far too often, with tit-for-tat abuse about the Munich and Istanbul tragedies, and people still search for the genesis. Wikipedia will tell you it stems from the War of the Roses and the industrial revolution, but it doesn't. There are various things that have fuelled it – hooliganism, the media's fawning over 'United' as if there is only one, the refusal to accept Revie's Leeds were capable of stunning football as well as a high tackle, McQueen, Jordan, Ferdinand, Smith. Manchester fans bang on about stealing Eric Cantona, forgetting Leeds stole Johnny Giles and Gordon Strachan. Yet Leeds' demise means it has been a rivalry largely unheard for 20 years. So they had not played for six years when League One Leeds went to the Premier League champions in 2010. Those involved explain what happened next.

MANCHESTER UNITED 0 LEEDS UNITED 1:
THE RIVALRY

BY JAMES RIACH

There was a moment, after the toil was over and the stands had emptied, that Sir Alex Ferguson caught Simon Grayson off guard.

'Do you understand pressure?' asked Ferguson, calmly and respectfully, even with the miasma of defeat lingering in his office. Confounded for a second, Grayson looked bemused, not offering a response until the question was repeated. 'To some extent,' he replied, 'but not to the level you do.'

Ferguson paused. 'Well, I've got money on you to get promoted, so you better see it through. That's pressure.'

Such was the endorsement that Grayson received as he supped white wine at Old Trafford – he declined red – in the aftermath of a victory that provided unbridled elation after so many seasons of misery. Promotion, though, was for another day. This, right now, was a memory to savour. It was a beam of light that broke through the dark clouds over Elland Road, clouds that had hung like Mordor murk for six years and only now were beginning to dissipate. It was a result that rippled across the country and provided Ferguson with his only third-round defeat in the FA Cup during his entire 26-year reign.

A one-off duel between Manchester United and Leeds is significant whatever the weather but, considering the context of January 2010, the events of that crisp Sunday have gone down in local folklore. Only a few weeks previously Leeds had needed a replay and extra time to overcome Kettering Town in the second round of the competition. In League One teams start the Cup in round one and the grim reality of the club's recent history meant that they were hoping to reach the third round and draw a big team, a situation which at one time would have been unthinkable. They had sunk low, and life in the third division was tough.

But despite the play-off defeats, the relegations, the administration, the points deduction . . . despite all the rancour, disappointment and spite, something felt different this year. Leeds were on course for a return to the Championship, unbeaten in 15 games before 3 January and with a talented squad packed with future Premier League players. In the end the campaign did not quite reach the serene denouement that at one stage seemed assured, but by the turn of the year they were on top of the table and playing with a swagger that belied their third-tier status.

Something felt different. Perhaps it was the form of Jermaine Beckford and Luciano Becchio, or the eminent durability of Richard Naylor and Patrick Kisnorbo, a central partnership that appeared the antidote to years of defensive fragility. Perhaps it was having a supporter as manager, a man who felt the highs and lows just as acutely as those stood at the Gelderd End. These were a few of the ingredients that ensured Leeds travelled across the Pennines to play the Premier League champions, a side ranked 42 places above them, with the utmost confidence in their ability to get a result. Certainly there was a stark awareness of the task in hand, bearing in mind Leeds' last two games had been against Hartlepool United and Stockport County, and seven months previously Manchester United had played Barcelona in a European Cup final. But, considering the chasm between the two, there was not the feeling of apprehension that there might have been.

'I remember the week leading up to it, what with the rivalry between Leeds and Man United,' recalls Michael Doyle, the midfielder who joined for the 2009–10 season on loan from Coventry City. 'It was a massive game for Leeds, having been away for so long and being down in League One. We knew it was a War of the Roses match, but from Man United's point of view I think they thought it was just a League One side. For us it was a massive game and a free hit, really.'

A shot-to-nothing, a chance to return on the big stage and prove there was still plenty of fight in the old dog, a dog that's tail had not wagged for some time. This was the time, this was the opportunity that the fans had been waiting for: the opportunity to forget Watford, to forget Doncaster, to forget Millwall; to forget the draining reality of the Football League and seize the day against the oldest of enemies. Yet there is something about this fixture that will always negate the idea of a 'free hit', whatever the situation. Numerous supporters boarded the trains early on Sunday morning at Leeds station with hope in their hearts but pragmatism in their heads, with an unspoken desire to simply not be on the end of a hiding, to be able to return with heads high and reputations intact. This was no mere one-off game, even in these unlikely circumstances: enmity between the two clubs still festered, as potent as ever, even if it had lain dormant since the last meeting in 2004.

'Everyone knows what Sir Alex is like,' recalls Grayson. 'He doesn't like losing many games – especially any against their biggest rivals.'

For Ferguson, it was a rivalry like no other. It was a mutual fire that had raged for decades, with the transfers of Eric Cantona and Alan Smith doing plenty to fan the flames of animosity during Ferguson's tenure. 'I have always said Liverpool–Manchester United games are fierce in many aspects,' he said in 2011. 'Sometimes supporters can play a bad

part in that particular game. But it never reaches the levels of
Leeds United. Never.'

Manchester United had undoubtedly held the upper hand
over Leeds during Ferguson's era and it is fair to say that he
was not regarded with much fondness by Leeds fans. Indeed,
he was once almost set upon outside Elland Road. 'This bunch
of supporters, skinheads, 20 or 30 of them, see me and go,
"Ferguson!" and start running across the road. The lights are
still red, I'm almost shitting myself, they're getting nearer, then
the light goes to amber and [impersonation of a tyre-squeal]
I'm away.'

With rivalries renewed and with an increased ticket allocation
meaning 9,000 Leeds supporters would be inside the stadium,
Greater Manchester Police regarded the game as a high-risk
occasion. An air of tension and expectancy hung over Old
Trafford as kick-off approached, with chants of 'we all hate
Leeds scum' sporadically breaking through the red hoards on
Sir Matt Busby Way ahead of the early start.

Grayson and his team were already *in situ* as the atmosphere
crackled, ready for this colossal tussle after a tranquil preparation
at nearby Mottram Hall. There was no trepidation during the
build-up, with the squad undergoing the same routines and
drills as if it were another league match.

'Simon put square pegs in square holes and he knew how
to get results,' says Andy Hughes, who started the game at left-
back. Simplicity, according to Hughes, was one of Grayson's
underlying successes, and the instructions were clearly
delivered. 'Grayson had a plan, he had a dream and he made it
really clear what the idea was. He made us believe we could get
something. There was a good feeling; there was no pressure on
us. Everything was really relaxed. We had a little meeting before
we left the hotel, he went through the team and the subs, said
to try to keep them quiet for the first 15 minutes and the crowd

would get on their backs. But "believe in yourself, no pressure. Go and enjoy it".'

That was the message Grayson relayed to his players, but internally he understood the epic scale of the game. Brian Flynn was the last player to score a winning goal for Leeds at Old Trafford in 1981, emphatically firing in a first-time effort for Allan Clarke's side, and the Welsh midfielder reminded Grayson of that feat a few weeks beforehand. More than any player in the squad, Grayson was aware of the history.

'We tried to treat it as a normal game but you just can't, going to Old Trafford and with the magnitude of it all. All the eyes were on us,' he says. 'We didn't go there with nothing to lose but we knew that we wanted to put on a performance. Some of the players knew it was one of the biggest games of their careers. I kept stressing to them that they could be a new batch of heroes that the fans could worship in the future.'

The team knew that if they were going to pull off a seismic shock then every single individual would need to fire. A minor injury meant Robert Snodgrass did not start, while Max Gradel was ineligible because of his loan contract. Other than that it would be the same XI that had outclassed most opponents during the season to date. Beckford was flying and Leeds were dreaming again. 'That squad that went up, we had top players that went on to bigger and better things,' says Hughes. 'We knew we had a team, but we were the underdogs for once.' Doyle remembers, 'We were full of confidence, we were playing good, attacking football that season. We never worked too much on shape – the manager was very old school in a sense. His approach was train hard, make training enjoyable and then, on a Friday, you'd just gear up for a game. We did a little bit of shape but it was our usual 4–4–2.'

During the pre-match build up on ITV, studio pundit Gareth Southgate said, 'I live in the heart of Leeds country, in the people's republic of Yorkshire. This is a big game. They are travelling more in hope than expectation, but with that glint in their eye, thinking, "Could we, could we do something today?"'

Even then, no one would really have believed what was to come. No one could have expected that in the 2010 General Election a man changed his name by deed poll to 'We Beat the Scum 1-0' in order to stand as a candidate in the Leeds Central constituency. And no one would have believed that 155 people decided to vote for him.

For most of Leeds' squad this was their first taste of Old Trafford. The exception was Doyle, who played an integral role in Coventry's League Cup win there in 2007. 'I'd played against Anderson before and won when I was at Coventry,' says Doyle. 'They were top players. They had a strong team out and there were some tackles flying in, to be fair. I remember before the game, outside the away dressing room, Gary Neville walking past with his chest puffed out. He looked like he was on a mission. I thought, "Bloody hell, he looks up for it today."'

If Grayson, Jonny Howson and Richard Naylor were the ones who knew what this meant from a Leeds perspective, then Neville and Wes Brown were the local lynchpins for the opposition. Ferguson selected a strong side, with Wayne Rooney and Dimitar Berbatov starting up front, and the notable absentees being Patrice Evra, Edwin van der Sar and Paul Scholes. Nemanja Vidić, a rock at centre-back, had pulled up injured during the warm-up. Nonetheless, it was a strong statement from Ferguson, a seemingly dangerous blend of youth and experience with the raw but talented 19-year-old Danny Welbeck on the wing.

Hughes says, 'We knew that they were having a go. You had them all, it wasn't like they were hiding, they weren't putting a weakened team out.' With a galvanised Neville and physical central midfield pairing of Anderson and Darren Gibson, any preconceptions Leeds may have had about Premier League fancy-Dans were quickly dispelled.

'When the game started I remember Wes Brown smashing into me, and I've still probably got the stud marks on my shin from when Gary Neville absolutely rinsed me,' says Doyle. 'I didn't want to show it at the time but I remember a big gash on my leg after the game. It was very competitive. They had players with pace and power, but we just went out, all guns blazing.'

Grayson's calm and diligent preparations proved fruitful as the game wore on, yet there were still understandable nerves beforehand. The Leeds goalkeeper, Casper Ankergren, had an injection in his shoulder and barely trained in the build-up, also struggling to obtain any meaningful rest on the Saturday night. 'People were quite relaxed, we were looking forward to going to Old Trafford. There was no pressure on us. But you can't enjoy a game where you get battered four or five nil, and that was one of the things that could have happened,' he says. 'We were a League One team, but a very good League One team. But we were playing against Manchester United from the Premier League, we knew they were going to put out a decent side, which they did. I had mixed feelings beforehand. I didn't sleep very well, I kept waking up thinking about the game – I'd never had it like that before. But as soon as I walked on the pitch I wasn't nervous. I just thought, "Here we go, let's give it our best." The manager just said, "Let's have a right good go and see where it takes us."'

A red banner with Cantona's face etched upon it alongside the taunting provocation 'Thanks a Million' was unfurled shortly before kick-off, stoking the atmosphere further. The Frenchman's name was sung by the home supporters as soon as referee Chris Foy blew his whistle to begin the match, but Leeds were not overawed. Instead, they delivered exactly on

Grayson's promise, frustrating Ferguson's side in the early stages by keeping tight and compact. The men in red may have enjoyed much of the possession in the opening 15 minutes but they could do little with it.

Then, the magic. The moment of delirium. The finest pass in a Leeds generation. The heavy first touch but sweetest of scuffs. The frustration and hurt, the goldfish, the CVAs, the reckless and the feckless, all forgotten in a moment of golden alchemy.

It all started with Brown at right centre-half, who played a long free-kick forward which Berbatov expertly controlled. Yet there was Naylor, who met the languid Bulgarian's fine touch with a strong dose of Yorkshire grit. The Leeds captain hassled his opponent off the ball, and the white orb soon fell under the control of young sorcerer Howson. What happened next was, according to Doyle, a 'World Cup pass' and, for Hughes, a 'worldy ball'. Grayson, watching on from the touchline, simply remembers, 'Jonny picked the pass like he can.'

Manchester United were playing an incredibly high line which, in retrospect, was their downfall. Given that Leeds' main threat was on the counterattack, with the pace of Beckford, allowing the former RAC windscreen-fitter a void of space behind the defence was a naïve approach gleefully exploited. Howson, 21 at the time, released a looping 60-yard pass from inside his own half that hung in the air like some great missile waiting to hone in on its target. It seemed like an age. The ball arced up, watched intently by the 74,000 inside the stadium, by Wilkinson, by Gray, by Lorimer and Flynn. Eventually it dropped at Beckford's feet, with Brown already in trouble. The defender was caught in an awful position, helplessly watching the ball drift over his head and into the path of his adversary. It was at this point that the Leeds supporters knew something was afoot. A guttural roar rose from the opposite end of the stadium as Beckford's eyes lit up. His first touch initially looked to have squandered the chance but goalkeeper Tomasz Kuszczak was hesitant. A hush suddenly descended on Old Trafford, and Beckford steered home with his left foot from a tight angle in front of the Stretford End.

'The best thing about the goal was that Becks actually scuffed it in, because I think if he'd have caught it well we wouldn't have scored,' says Hughes. 'As soon as it went to Jermaine we all had a feeling United were in trouble, with the form he had been in that season. When it hit the back of the net, at the Stretford End, it was brilliant.' Grayson was equally thankful of the finish: 'It's one of those, if Jermaine had caught it cleanly Kuszczak would have probably saved it. But when you see it rolling past him you think, "Wow, have we just gone 1-0 up at Old Trafford?"'

There are few moments that stand out so prominently in the memory for a younger generation of Leeds supporters, those who may not even remember the Champions League run at the start of the millennium. This would leave an indelible mark, a gloriously simple and beautiful goal coming in the game of games. 'It gave us something to hold onto,' says Doyle, who knew that he and the Leeds defence would now be subjected to a stringent examination for the remaining 70 minutes. Soon after going ahead, right-back Jason Crowe cleared a Rooney effort off the line, but Leeds more than held their own during the opening half. 'The manager was really relaxed at half-time,' says Hughes. 'He said, "You deserve it, you can get another one. Be brave."'

Grayson had said in his pre-match interview that Leeds were not going to be intimidated by their opponents, that they were going to have a 'right good go'. It was this mental fortitude that shone through as the game progressed: a steadfast desire not to crumble when under pressure, to keep playing their own game, not the opposition's. It would have been easy at this juncture to sit back, to protect the advantage, to capitalise on the discontent that was beginning to emanate from the stands as Foy signalled for half-time. But Grayson knew that history did not favour such an approach at Old Trafford. This was Ferguson's turf, the place where many a side had capitulated late on despite performing admirably for much of the match. To avoid that fate, Leeds needed to keep their composure.

'I don't think the pressure in the first half was too bad, to be honest with you, they had half-chances, but nothing much,' says Ankergren. 'In the second half it started building and became a lot of pressure, but we had Naylor and Kisnorbo at centre-back. We had a good back four which enjoyed being under pressure and just defending. When we were 1-0 up at half-time I was still a little bit pessimistic. I've been up 1-0 at half-time before and lost. But we kept going and I started to think, "OK . . ."'

The strange thing was, while Manchester United did have chances to equalise, Leeds were not under siege until the very last seconds. It was as if time had been reversed, as if this was one of the great, even contests of old. Such was the compelling ebb and flow of the second half that it was easy to forget how this was a League One team against the Premier League champions. There was still an expectation in the crowd that a goal would come, that order would be restored. But as the minutes went by, anxiety and fear grew. Surely this was not actually going to happen? Surely someone in a red shirt would squash these impudent third division saboteurs who were foolishly unaware how teams were expected to behave at Old Trafford?

Ankergren was called into action, saving well to deny Welbeck before keeping Berbatov out from close range. Ferguson had not made any substitutions at half-time but by 57 minutes he played his gambit: Ryan Giggs and Antonio Valencia were brought on for Welbeck and Gabriel Obertan, before Michael Owen replaced Anderson. Doyle recalls, 'I wouldn't say it was backs to the wall but we had to defend. I just remember Valencia knocking the ball past Hughesy at one stage, leaving him for absolute dead.'

Leeds were still a threat themselves, as Beckford pulled one wide on the break and Snodgrass – introduced in the 77th minute for Howson – shook the angle of post and crossbar with a free-kick from just outside the D. The only real concern at this point was whether they would pay the ultimate price for these near misses, that they would feel the pain of profligacy. A replay at Elland Road would, before the game, have been considered a diamond result. But now, with victory so close, anything less became unthinkable. Ankergren had to be alert to thwart Owen in a late goalmouth scramble, as the finishing tape drew nearer and Ferguson's eyes burned into his charges with a desperate intent. 'I don't think they caused us too many problems,' says Grayson. 'Casper wasn't having to pull too many saves out of the bag. But it wasn't until the fourth official put the board up that you realised you were only a few minutes away.'

It was at that point, when five additional minutes were signalled, that Leeds' resolve truly shone. There was still time for Kisnorbo – bandaged and bloodied – to throw himself in front of a Gibson shot, and still time for Rooney to fire at Ankergren and then wide. These were the minutes when game-plans were exchanged for sheer mettle, when every bounce and ricochet was met with a gasp. But the ball never did fall for a man in red, and the home fans knew that disaster was imminent: many were already heading home before Foy blew his whistle for the last time, drawing the curtain on a performance for the ages.

'I don't think at the time I quite knew how big the game was for the fans,' says Ankergren. 'It was only afterwards that I realised what it meant.' This was a sentiment supported by Hughes, who had worked tirelessly to secure the clean sheet:

'We came off the pitch with a sense of "we actually deserved that". It wasn't a fluke,' he recalls. 'I don't think any of us knew what it really meant until the next day. A League One team had beaten one of the biggest teams in world football. But albeit, we were Leeds United, one of the biggest teams in the world still. It was fantastic to see all the fans and family.'

The scenes at full-time were, in many ways, a prolonged form of catharsis. The ecstasy lasted not just for minutes, or even hours, but for many days. One has to remember that this was no ordinary win, not even an ordinary derby win. For so long Leeds supporters had suffered the baiting and goading from rivals yet, for a brief time at least, roles were reversed. People turned up for work in the following week with beaming grins, remembering that this – these feelings – was why they loved football. It had been an unrequited love for so many years but now, in the haze of this wonderful, wonderful success, all the sacrifices and heartache were worth it. Doyle recalls how 'all the Leeds fans in the coaches afterwards were going absolutely barmy', while Ankergren even managed to earn a free takeaway: 'I went to McDonald's the day after and got some free food. The guy recognised me and said, "You beat Man United yesterday, you can have this for free." Everybody remembers that game. People will always remember it; it will always stay with me. As a single game it was probably my best experience.'

Ferguson was stunned but full of praise for Leeds, saying they fought 'like tigers', adding, 'Human beings can always surprise you but I didn't expect that.' Grayson, on the other hand, was intent on remembering the moment, absorbing the emotions of the players and the adulation of the supporters. He says, 'We celebrated with the 9,000 fans. I wanted to take our time, so we walked slowly along the touchline. I said to Paul Dews, the head of media, who was trying to hurry me along to the press room, "We've got to soak this up. Let's make this the slowest walk you've ever done, because it might not come around for a long time.'"

Grayson was right. He delivered promotion that season but was sacked by Ken Bates in February 2012, citing the wins at Old Trafford and against Bristol Rovers on the last day of the 2009–10 campaign as his defining triumphs. However, in the aftermath of this strenuous and exhausting game, there was a hangover. League form suffered as the club became enthralled by the possibility of an extended Cup run. Leeds were drawn against Tottenham in the fourth round but before then were held at home by Wycombe Wanderers and beaten at Exeter City, also being thrashed 3-0 by Swindon Town three days after a 2-2 draw at White Hart Lane. If anything, the win at Old Trafford derailed the promotion focus, as Leeds won only two matches in 12 after Spurs knocked them out of the Cup in a 3-1 replay at Elland Road on 3 February. By that point the prospect of another torturous play-off finale had significantly dampened the mood, as the confidence of earlier in the season began to wane.

Yet this was always going to be a year to remember. Clawing their way out of League One, out of the quagmire, had to be done. Another campaign in the third division would have killed the momentum that the victory at Old Trafford promised – the new dawn after living the nightmare. It was left until the final day, against Bristol Rovers, as Beckford and Howson came to the fore once more, when Leeds secured a dramatic slice of redemption.

Hughes says, 'Winning at Man United was part of the journey. I always think successful teams who have a successful year, something always happens in the season, like a Cup run. It was a day I'll never forget. We'd been through a lot with the minus 15 points and the play-off defeat with Gary Mac.

'The season had everything – the last game with Max Gradel getting sent off and down to ten men, but still winning promotion. That could only happen at Leeds United. There was a sense of relief. I was the first player to go there when they got 15 points deducted, and I'd set a target to get out of that league. To finally do it, there was that sense of relief, which is why I ran towards the Kop. I've seen the picture and the relief – it's the world to me, it really is.'

That team will always be remembered fondly by Leeds supporters, not only for winning at Old Trafford but for injecting new life into the club. Since the Championship play-off final humbling against Watford in 2006 no manager had been able to craft any kind of team identity. Squads were fragmented, players came and went with alarming rapidity, and the relationship between the club and fans suffered. 2009–10 changed that. As Harry Redknapp, the Tottenham manager, said after Beckford had scored twice in north London, Leeds' team 'could go through a league next year and it could carry them into the Premier League easily. They could be back where they were'.

That never did transpire, though, as one by one the stars of that Cup run were prised away. It is arguably one of the biggest travesties in Leeds' recent history that a squad packed with such potential only fulfilled that potential elsewhere. Grayson's side finished seventh the following season and missed out on a play-off spot by three points. It felt at the time like a major disappointment but it was not for another six years that Leeds, under Garry Monk, resembled genuine promotion contenders again. After Grayson's departure the next five Championship finishing positions were 14th, 13th, 15th, 15th and 13th.

Yet even though Manchester United 0-1 Leeds United on 3 January 2010 did not become the true springboard that many hoped it would, the victory created tighter bonds and lasting camaraderie within a squad that needed every ounce of unity on the final day of the season. History may view Leeds' elevation from League One to the Championship as a formality, something that was always going to happen due to the size and stature of the club. But at the time it felt like a giant weight had finally been lifted, that rock-bottom had been hit and overcome, that things would never be quite as bad again.

'I've always tried to treat the players like they're my friends, without over-stepping the mark and taking it too far,' says Grayson. 'We did feel like it was a special group that could grow and flourish together over a number of years, which unfortunately wasn't allowed to happen. They were talented, they were hard working in training and we tried to create a spirit amongst the group where they related to each other. You had lots of unsung heroes, like Patrick Kisnorbo, Richard Naylor and Andy Hughes, who were just great lads to work with. They knew their jobs within the group and were really appreciated by the other lads who could go and win us games. Even now I stay in touch with a lot of people from that group.'

As for the rivalry with Manchester United, a 3-0 defeat at Elland Road in the League Cup in 2011 was at least some revenge for Ferguson in his final game against Leeds. That result will never be immortalised, however. Only one game against Manchester United will be sung about for years to come, only one date will always remembered.

'I was immensely proud of how the staff set the team up and our preparations, then the players carried out what we asked them to do,' says Grayson. 'Sir Alex Ferguson was really good afterwards. We had a few staff in his room and he was very respectful. He said, "You deserved that, credit to your players." I look back at it from a personal point of view, that my team had gone to Old Trafford and beaten Sir Alex Ferguson's team. That's what I look back on.'

7

Arguably the finest full-back to play for Leeds United, the Australian-born **Tony Dorigo** was a key component of the 1992 title-winning side. Fast, deceptively strong and with a tasty shot, he also had the misfortune to room with David Batty, as you will discover below. Dorigo cost Leeds £1.3 million from Chelsea when that got you a lot more than your own name tattooed on your forehead in Sanskrit. Here he tells his story in detail, from being pitched into inner-city Birmingham as a 15-year-old to scoring at Wembley and being the player of the year at four different cubs. Ken Bates, Eric Cantona and Marilyn Manson feature.

TONY DORIGO: EASY

BY RICK BROADBENT

There is a hierarchy in football that is born in the playground. Fancy Dan girl-magnets with manicured hair are the strikers. Fey aesthetes with breadstick legs and a back catalogue of Nick Drake albums are wingers. Borstal boys and manual labourers are natural centre-halves. Goalkeepers are useless or psychotic, often both. Full-backs, though, are inherently lacking in glamour, aspiring to nothing more than a decent slide tackle or a ball down the channel. In truth, nobody really wants to be a full-back. Even in these days of wing-backs, it remains a modest ambition, which is why I am surprised when Tony Dorigo tells me he was player of the year at Leeds United in 1992.

Those who can remember a halcyon time before Ken Bates and *Love Island* will know 1992 was no ordinary year. Indeed, it may never be repeated. Middle-aged men still gush about that perfect midfield – the gilded passes of Gary McAllister, the ginger genius of Gordon Strachan, the beef dripping simplicity of David Batty (see the Billy Bragg line in 'A Lover Sings' – 'There is no real substitute for a ball struck firmly and squarely') and the hair and flair of Gary Speed. Up front Lee Chapman scored 16 league goals with a mesmerising economy of movement. At the back Chris Whyte was a revelation. Yet, the player of the year, *this year*, was the left-back. Maybe it was because it all just looked a bit easy for a club fuelled by suffering.

'The game was too easy for him,' Strachan once agreed. 'Maybe it was the way he looked, his hair all neatly in place, the fact he was never dirty. I was very happy with his effort but always felt he had another 10 per cent to give.'

We are meeting in the sort of chic Leeds hotel that Leeds never used to have – Dorigo is living back in the city now – and it seems Strachan has a point. Dorigo has scarcely changed, looking sleek in a black jumper, although he says he refuses to play football now but can cope with cycling and the gym. The hair is a little thinner, but not much, and is certainly neat. During our conversation he is interrupted by a Liverpool fan, and kindly commiserates about the Champions League final, and then by Scott Sellars, who he greets like a lost friend, in precisely the way we fans always hope old Leeds players would do. He is nice, polite, says he is still 'talking rubbish' on TV and the only hint of a dark side comes when he tells me his son, Todd, a singer-songwriter and guitarist, has toured with his band INK on the same bill as goat-eyed Goth crooner Marilyn Manson.

Yet he soon kills the idea that he had it easy as he recalls moving from Australia, the madness of Ken Bates, being bombarded with coins when he held aloft the European Cup, and the risks of rooming with Batty.

'Strach says that, but the thing is, some players look like they are working really hard and others don't,' he says. 'I said to him, "It's like a duck – everything looks serene on the surface but, underneath, those legs are going like the clappers." I was up and down that wing and he thinks I'm a Rolls Royce, but I'm human. Eddie Gray said the same thing to me. He said I played for Leeds with a cigar for five years, but I really didn't. It wasn't easy.'

Take those times spent in the company of Leeds' much-loved destroyer. He recounts the example of Batty's local-hero status mentioned earlier by Anthony Clavane. 'Batts was a local lad, which I soon came to realise meant a huge amount in these parts. Everyone likes one of their own, of course, but the scale of it became apparent to me when we played Man City at home [September 1991]. I scored a really good goal from around 25 yards, a sweet half-volley bent into the top corner. Then Batts scored. It was not quite a tap in, but I swear the roof came off Elland Road. It registered on the Richter scale, and even the hairs on the back of my neck were going. I thought, "What the hell is going on?" Then came the interviews. We'd won 3-0 and I was waiting, thinking they were going to ask me about my amazing goal. The first question was, "What do you think about Batts' goal?" It was great for him, great for the fans and, as a teammate, you wouldn't want anyone else alongside you in the trenches, but . . .'

Trenches are one thing, but a hotel room is another, and Dorigo shines a light on what might most politely be termed the enigmatic side of Battyness: 'I got on really well with him, but at certain times his personality would shine through. It was like that when we were away with England in Malaysia. Club-mates often got lumped together and we were sharing. We had a day off and I was going to play golf and he went off fishing. That night he came back and his tracksuit was absolutely covered in fish guts. There was blood everywhere and he stunk. I said, "Your tracksuit is flipping disgusting." He just looked at me and said, "It's not mine, it's yours." Then he took it off and gave it to me. I thought, "What the hell, is this a joke?"'

Another occasion, another England camp, and Batty clashed with Keith Curle, a man not slow in backing down himself, and someone with a tendency to tackle like a tobogganing Orc. 'He broke Curley's jaw in training, accidentally,' Dorigo says. 'The next day Curley comes out of hospital, in Australia, and he is eating through a straw. All the lads are laughing. Batts is sitting with me in the dining hall when Curley comes over and sits down with us. Everyone is waiting for Batts to say "sorry", or something. Nothing. Awkward. He finished up and went to his room. There were never any airs or graces. What you see is what you get.'

Yet it is worth noting that Batty, arguably the most loved of all players by Leeds folk, had it easier. Strachan, Gray and perhaps all those fans who voted him player of the year in 1992 did not appreciate the journey Dorigo had taken to get to the top.

'My father was Italian and emigrated to Australia when he was 15 and became an Australian citizen. My mum is Australian. I played for Adelaide City and was training with the first team when I was 15. I was watching English football on *Star Soccer* and wondering how I was going to keep progressing if I was already with the first team at that age. I could not speak Italian so I could not go there. Then Justin Fashanu came over on loan and I asked him lots of questions about England. He was fantastic and said he could help me out at Norwich City, but I sat down one day and wrote a letter to 12 clubs. I got one letter back, from Aston Villa, offering a four-day trial, and so I came over with my dad. I turned up to their training ground at Bodymoor Heath and I'll never forget it. I was up against apprentices who were 16 and 17, the ball was whizzing this way and that, and I could not get near it. But they said I could stay for another week. Then they said they wanted to sign me, but I was too young. I said I'd go back to Australia for school, but they said, "You're not going anywhere."

'It was amazing. There were no real precedents for an Australian kid. John Kosmina had come over but found it too cold for him and he went home [he made one substitute appearance for Arsenal against Leeds in 1978], but now a kid from Australia was at a club like Villa, who were flying. They won the old First Division in 1981 and then the European Cup in 1982. It was a great time to be there but the downside was school.

'I went to Aston Manor, an inner-city school, and it was one of the worst winters on record. I made the front page of the local paper, waiting by myself at a bus stop in the snow when no buses were running. It was a tough school. I had my sheepskin coat and Aussie boots. I did not have to do metalwork so I'd catch up on geography – because I only knew it from an Australian view – and I'd sit at the back watching some lad looking at me as he sharpened a knife. I thought I better get these people on my side.'

Dorigo stuck it out in a chaotic house of wannabes overseen by the Villa kit man and progressed from schoolboy forms to a £20-a-week apprentice deal, complete with free travel card. He looked after the boots of Gordon Cowans, a Pirlo-esque midfielder, and Jimmy Rimmer, the goalkeeper, who was the anal side of pedantic, with six pairs of boots for every meteorological shift. Rimmer, who had been on the bench when Manchester United won the European Cup in 1968, famously re-injured his shoulder ten minutes into the 1982 final against Bayern Munich. Nigel Spink's heroics effectively prompted the end of Rimmer's reign, and thanks to a Dutch divot and Peter Withe's shin, Dorigo found himself holding the European Cup ahead of the first game of the following season.

'Me and David Norton, another apprentice, paraded the trophy around Villa Park before the first game of the season,' he recalls. 'Foolishly, we walked in front of the Sunderland supporters and suddenly it was "ping, ping, ping". All these coins were bouncing off the European Cup. That was an eye-opener.'

Dorigo signed as a professional when he was 17. Villa had peaked and after finishing sixth in 1983 they slid into mid-table before an inevitable relegation. Yet Dorigo's star was in the ascendant and he bagged his first player of the year award. 'I'd gone from nothing to playing at Old Trafford and Highbury. Then I got the player of the year. Everything was great, and then they tried to sell me. Doug Ellis called me and said he was going to pick me up in a couple of hours and take me to London because Chelsea wanted to buy me. What should I do?

I was devastated. I could not believe it. This was crazy. But that year we were struggling to score goals and Villa wanted David Speedie. Chelsea said the only way they were getting him was if they got Dorigo. It ended up like a Mexican stand-off in the Post House Hotel. There was Ken Bates and Speedie on one side of the corridor and me and Deadly Doug on the other. Speedie got released and walked into the middle and we both went into our different rooms to negotiate. Speedie said no and I refused to sign. We got out of there quick. I didn't go back with Doug that night. It could have been awkward. I realised then that you are a commodity.'

When Billy McNeill achieved the remarkable feat of relegating Manchester City and Villa in the same season, it was a matter of time before Dorigo would be offloaded. Graham Taylor then arrived and Dorigo remembers the first Churchillian address full of 'claret and blue running through our veins' and the like. 'Then he said, "Whoever does not want to be here, there's the door." He then turned around and said, "And you, Dorigo, if you want to go to Chelsea then the deal is done." The thing is, he was pointing at Gary Williams! I would not have thought of leaving, but Chelsea were in the top division, I had England ambitions, and so off I went.'

Off into the heart of London, the yin to Leeds' yang since Sniffer was playing carpet bowls and Raquel Welch was waddling down the touchline at Stamford Bridge shouting 'yoo-hoo' at Peter Osgood. The 1970 FA Cup final and the maiming of Eddie Gray had lit a touch-paper which the concerted efforts of old-school ultras then doused in paraffin as they bridged the north–south divide with hardcore hooliganism. One thing that the clubs also have in common, unfortunately, is Kenneth William Bates.

'Chelsea was different,' Dorigo says. 'In Leeds football is everything, but in London there are so many things. It's easy to get lost. I found the fans fantastic but I had gone from a team struggling on the pitch to one that was chaotic off it. There was so much influence from Mr Bates that affected players. Poor old John Hollins [the manager] spent six weeks meticulously working out his pre-season, getting the players in, fine-tuning the squad, working out the system, and then, an hour before the first game of the season, Bates sends the chief executive down with a load of papers to sign. We had just had the team talk and he says, "Can you quickly sign these?" We all wanted to know what we were signing, of course, and it turned out we were agreeing to a £600 deduction from our wages as a form of income tax. We were all like, "What the bloody hell is this?" There was flipping uproar. We should have been going out for the warm-up and we were still in our suits. We almost went on strike. We told the chief exec to piss off and he ran back up to Bates. Poor Holly had to deal with this stuff all the time. What chance did we have when we had to deal with this sort of rubbish? We had some really good players but we could win seven on the trot and lose seven. There was too much interference from Bates. We got relegated, promoted, and I had one of the best days in my career when we won the Zenith Data Systems Trophy against Boro. OK, not a big deal, maybe, but there were 74,000 people there and I scored from a free-kick in the top corner. It was not like now – Chelsea hadn't been to Wembley for years. And the players did not get a bonus in any of the rounds. On the last day, Holly said there would be £500 for a win, but he was paying it from his own pocket because the chairman wouldn't. It was a farce. You'd see someone with a face on one day and something would have happened.

'Rangers came in for me and I asked for a transfer. I went in to see Bates and said I did not think we were rowing in the same direction and could not see us winning big things. He showed me my contract. "You have two years left – there's the door."

'I was angry but I always gave 100 per cent, and so I played out my contract. Rangers were still talking but Leeds came in quickly and hard. Good old Bill Fotherby drove me around Leeds, and Wilko seemed a genuine guy. I'd played at Elland Road and, Jeez, the atmosphere was hot. Leeds had finished fourth that year. Vinnie had gone. McAllister and Strachan were there. Steve Hodge, Rod Wallace, I'm thinking we have pace and ability, then there's Batty and Speedo. This looks good.'

The first meeting with Howard Wilkinson, often stereotyped as a flat-capped monotone somewhere between dinosaur and whippet breeder, defied expectations. Wilkinson, having brushed up on Dorigo's extracurricular activities, knew he liked golf and embarked on an extended metaphor: 'We played three holes verbally, which was weird. He said, "There's a stream 270 yards down the fairway and you can hit it 300, but why go in the stream? Take a three-wood and go short. Don't muscle it." Now, I like golf, but stop it. I'm thinking, "Are we going to play 18 holes? Just give me the contract. I'll sign." I think he was just trying to say you need the right mix.'

Leeds paid £1.3 million for Dorigo and he fitted like a glove. Blisteringly quick, with an eye for goal and a nurtured love of defending, it did look easy. 'You'll never beat Dorigo' was a familiar chant, and that left-side combo with Gary Speed will probably never be surpassed at Elland Road. Yet, once again, looks can be deceptive, the submerged legs were flailing, and his start was a troubled one.

'Wilko came across as dour, obviously, but there was a sense of humour there, even if you had to dig deep to find it. Before I had even played for Leeds I had to have a double hernia operation, and so I flew back from the England camp in Malaysia. It normally took six weeks to recover but I only had five. A couple of weeks of rehab later Howard had me in his office. I could hardly walk. He said, 'Normally it takes six weeks but with you being a soft Aussie I'm wondering how long it will take you."

'I'm wondering if he's serious. Then he said, "Nigel Worthington came back in four and a half at Sheffield Wednesday." I'm wondering what he was getting at, but ended up saying, "Jesus, if you are used to Nigel Worthington wait until you see me." I said I'd be back in four. Then he started laughing. He could be intimidating.

'I thought we could improve on fourth but I didn't know by how much. Strach was the leader. He would watch every single game [back, afterwards] and if the young lads didn't then there would be a bollocking. He was ahead of the curve on diet, and for someone so small to have such a big influence was impressive. The project was great for him and gave him a boost at the right time. Everyone listened to him.

'Speedo was fantastic too. Him and Batts were the two muckers, the two youngsters. As a left-back, my god, he was a dream to play with. He would listen to everything you said and get back in position defensively. He could do everything, go past people, score, head, was so down to earth and always wanted to learn. Later in my career at Torino, I briefly had the former most expensive player in the world playing right in front of me, but I would much rather have had Gary Speed than Gianluigi Lentini.

'In defence we had two of the most honest centre-halves. I'm not saying they were the best at every part of the game – they were not going to beat players and ping 50-yard balls – but they spilled blood. And then we had a goalkeeper who never worried you. Anything floating in the air a foot too high and I knew he'd come and get it. We did so many drills on the training ground that, as much as it bored us to death, we became proud to defend.

'The balance of the team was just right. Up front we had Chappie, tall and awkward but not that quick, and Rod, who was short and lightning-quick. In midfield we had Gary McAllister, tall and elegant, pinging passes for fun, alongside pitbull Batts, short and stuck in. Then at full-back we had the good-looking skinny one, and Mel Sterland.'

This is a half-joke as Dorigo clearly loved playing with the perennially perspiring Sterland, for whom the game never looked effortless. 'The most overused phrase on the bench that season was, "Get back, Mel!"' Dorigo says, but this was a multifaceted team whose munificence would match Man United, who were trying to win their first title for a quarter of a century.

New Leeds went ten games before they lost to a Mark Bright goal at Crystal Palace. The nation was watching. In the pre-Sky era [yes, kids, football existed before Jeff Stelling] live TV audiences watched Leeds thrash Aston Villa 4-1 and Sheffield Wednesday 6-1.

Yet by the time Strachan turned 35 in February 1992 it seemed that both he and Leeds might finally be hitting the wall. Wilkinson decided the answer was taking a little-known Frenchman called Eric Cantona on loan from Nîmes while Trevor Francis dithered at Sheffield Wednesday. Cantona always seemed an unlikely bedfellow for the authoritarian approach of Wilkinson, given he had already been banned from the French national side for calling the manager 'a shitbag' and had, in fact, quit international football before he arrived in Yorkshire. When encouraging supporters turned up in full Vietnam combat gear in homage to Cantona's hero, it took a while for them to appreciate this was a footballer who knew the difference between muscled-up killer Rambo and the absinthe-addled poet Arthur Rimbaud.

The 25-year-old hardly made the most auspicious of starts. His debut at Oldham on 8 February coincided with Leeds' second league defeat of the season and a dismal run in which they won three of their next 12 games. A 4-0 trouncing at Maine Road left the other Manchester club top of the table with three games in hand.

'I knew about Eric because I'd played against him for England under-21s at Highbury,' Dorigo says. 'He scored both. I thought, "He's a bit tasty" but then did not hear much until he turned up at Sheffield. I keep asking Trevor Francis about it and he says, "No, no, it was not a trial, he was here for a few days, the pitches were icy, he hardly played." He came to us for his first training session and scored a goal that I still find hard to believe. It was eight v eight, with the goals on the 18-yard lines. The keeper had thrown it over-arm out to the halfway line. Eric was running out towards the right-hand side and, as it dropped over his shoulder, he volleyed it 40 yards into the far top corner. I thought he'd miscontrolled it at first. Everyone stopped, stunned. Normally, if you score a goal like that you run around like an idiot, but he just jogged back to the halfway line and said, "We start again?" I thought, "Crying out loud, is that normal for you? We have got something here." He was also French and we understood what he could do and wouldn't do. He would not track back, and wanted to be the fulcrum of our attacking play. I think that is where him and the manager did not get on. Eric wanted an arm round him and made to feel important, whereas our side was built on 11 individuals doing their job rightly, so it becomes 11, not ten and a half. But we didn't feel that was a huge problem, because we could do that little bit extra because he could do the same at the other end.'

The importance of Cantona to Leeds' title has been revised in light of what he went on to achieve at Old Trafford. Strachan told me, 'Eric helped. He scored a few goals and gave us a bit extra, although, to be honest, you can over-emphasise his influence. I mean, I don't recall him scoring too many clinchers or setting anybody up for the winner.'

He made six starts and scored three goals but he did provide renewed hope when Leeds were staggering. 'He was not a huge influence,' Dorigo says. 'He came on and scored an amazing goal against Chelsea. It was what he went on to do that made people think he did more. He was a small part, an important part, but small. He could also lose the ability to understand English when he wanted. We took him out and never had an ounce of a problem with him, but it was his way; there was no other way. In the end it broke down. He wanted to go back to France. We were in London and he wasn't playing. He couldn't understand English again.

'Nobody could see what he would go on to do. Not to that extent. But if he had stayed at Leeds, would it have been the same? I can say no to that too. He was like the pied piper at Man United. They had six or seven youngsters who needed someone like that, just as Leeds needed Strachan. At Old Trafford he had all these youngsters who were going to work so hard for him and look up to him. You could see how that would work. A lot of people fail at Old Trafford because they cannot take it all in, but Eric was made for that stage.' Wilkinson would re-assess Cantona's influence with typical pithiness: 'Eric likes to do what he likes when he likes. And then he fucks off.'

But in the spring of 1992 all that lay ahead. Leeds were going toe-to-toe with Man United for the title and the only man who did not seem unduly worried was Dorigo: 'I never felt panic. None whatsoever. The big thing was the home games and what the crowd did. As that season went on we beat teams in the first ten minutes, psychologically. It was a two-way thing. We gave something to the crowd and they gave us something back. That's where Batty came in. Often you look back and he would do something in the first few minutes – a crunching tackle, probably – and the crowd went wild. It built and built. I do a sliding tackle on a winger, the crowd sing, "You'll never beat Dorigo" and I'm seven feet tall.

'Not every crowd does that. It was that time in history. Leeds were on a crest and going up and up. The crowd could never stay like that for ever. They were hungry and hungrier that year. It was a big help for us. If, as an opponent, you go to Elland

Road and, say, you've lost three on the spin, then someone smacks you and the crowd go crazy, then you have to react. There is no doubt about it that, at that time, it was something unique to overcome. And I knew what we could do as a team. I remember things, like a goal at Sheffield Wednesday.'

The goal he mentions, typically, is not his honey-sweet strike into the roof of the net from a well-worked free-kick, but the blink-and-you miss it brilliance of another: 'John Lukic thew the ball out to me on the left. I found Speedo down the wing first time. He took one touch to take it away from the defender and curled a beautiful cross for Chapman to score with a header. Four touches. People might say that was direct football, but it wasn't. It was class football: intricate, precise passing that was impossible to defend against.'

Bad run binned, Leeds finished strongly after seeing off Chelsea 3-0. Manchester United began to struggle simultaneously, prompting some tainted revisionism in which players and pundits said they blew the title rather than Leeds winning it. They even named Gary Pallister players' player of the year. Gary Lineker was the football writers' player of the year. Dorigo, though, was Leeds' player.

It came down to the penultimate weekend and Leeds would win their first title since 1974 if they beat Sheffield United at Bramall lane and Manchester United failed to get past Liverpool later in the day.

It was, as Dorigo says, a 'crazy' game, with 'a swirling wind and crisp wrappers flying' over the scuffed-up pitch. Leeds fell behind to a goal from Wimbledon throwback Alan Cork, but equalised through Wallace's deflected strike. Then fate began not so much to smile on Leeds as laugh hysterically. The Blades keeper, Mel Rees, suffered an injury and could only hobble around for the second half. That enabled Jon Newsome to stoop and conquer at the back post. An own goal by Chapman restored parity but then Cantona broke. He was challenged by

Brian Gayle and the ball bounced into the air. As Rees left his line with a semi-arthritic shuffle, Gayle headed the ball back over the keeper's head and into his own net.

Liverpool won 2-0 to seal the title for Leeds, although they would have won it a week later when they beat Norwich 1-0. 'It's the amount of points you get, not when you get them,' Strachan pointed out to Rain City miserablists. 'There were some great games and we played some great football. Nobody can dispute that.'

Dorigo did not pay much attention to the press during the run-in or afterwards: 'I learnt that early on when I played for Chelsea at Southampton. Kenny Sansom was the England left-back but there was a big push for me in the press for some reason. In the first ten minutes the ball hit my shin and I sliced one into the crowd. It was just one of those days when nothing went right. I picked up the paper the next morning and it said, "Man of the match – Dorigo: England class." I knew then not to get too carried away when you're up or when you're down. We won 6-1 at Sheffield Wednesday but we hadn't won anything. I tried to keep it on those terms.

'Howard was so detailed, so pragmatic. At other clubs we worked on set-pieces but at Leeds we went two steps beyond. We were doing defensive third, mid-third, attacking third, attacking and defending throw-ins. I was involved in a lot so I had to remember about 50 things. Batts would get so bored that we would send him away. It worked, though. When you're mentally fatigued at Old Trafford, hanging on for grim life, we would instinctively go into our corner positions because we had done it so often. We never switched off.

'Sheffield United was the weirdest day – weird weather, weird things happening – but I always felt we could handle weird things. Me and Batts were going off to England the next day to play in Russia. We had to meet in London, so I went to my in-laws in the midlands and watched the Liverpool game unfold. Some of the lads were all together, watching on a sofa, which seemed odd. Then I got a call from the boss, Howard. He was half-cut and said he'd had a call from the England manager and we didn't need to go with England. I drove back from the midlands and the next night we all met up. I think it was the Flying Pizza.

'We still had a game to go against Norwich, and we had to win that. But suddenly the legs did not feel like they were working properly. Rod scored a good goal and we got the job done. We won by four points in the end.'

The following season was awful. At Anfield that year the Kop stuck the knife in and chanted, 'You're not champions any more.' Leeds did not win away from home all year. Europe also ended prematurely – a great start against Rangers undone in rapid time. In truth, many of us were happy enough. Two titles in two years was sufficient to sate the starved.

'Ibrox was an amazing noise,' Dorigo says. 'There were no Leeds fans, but what a din. They billed it "the Battle of Britain", and I almost found myself singing, "We are the Billy Boys." I shouted something at Chris Fairclough eight yards away but he couldn't hear me. The only time we could communicate was after Gary McAllister scored that great goal. Then you could hear a pin drop. It was surreal. Then big John made a mistake and, to be fair, they played well after that and then got us early at Elland Road.

'The first round against Stuttgart had been amazing too. We lost the first leg 3-0 but battered them at home. At 4-1 we were out on away goals, but they fielded an ineligible player so we ended up having a play-off in an empty Nou Camp. There we were, playing the champions of Germany, in Barcelona, in such a big game, and our fans were not there. It was such a shame. I felt for Carl Shutt. He scored the winner and went running away to absolutely no one – the biggest moment of his career.'

In March 1995 Strachan went to Coventry. That year Lee Chapman dropped down a tier to play for Portsmouth. Worse still Batty, unthinkably, was sold. It was over, although there was the novelty of a Wembley appearance, the first since 1973 if we discount Charity Shield jousts with Liverpool.

'I missed the '96 Coca-Cola Cup final because I tore my hamstring on the morning of the game,' Dorigo says. 'I'd pulled it in the semi and trained all week at Bisham Abbey before the final. Speedo was desperate for me to be fit because if I didn't make it he was going to have to play left-back. I can still see him, "Tony, please." One last sprint and it went. It was one of our worst performances. [Savo] Milošević scored a great goal and we were soundly beaten. The only good thing was Andy Gray, who came in because of my injury and was our best player. We never reached those heights again. It was sad but inevitable when Howard went. He looked like a man who had the world on his shoulders. We were going nowhere.

'George Graham came in and I was offered a new contract, but it was very much appearance-based and it chopped my wage down. As much as I wanted to stay I had offers for a lot more. I thought Leeds could have offered a bit extra, but they wouldn't. I thought I was going to Boro, but then Graeme Sounness said, "Do you want to come to Italy?" and I jumped.'

Torino are one of Europe's forgotten clubs, long since overshadowed by city cousins Juventus, but home to one of sport's most tragic tales. In 1948 the 31 passengers and crew died when their aeroplane crashed into a hill at Superga, where an 18th century basilica stood above Turin. The dead included the Torino team that had not lost at home for 93 games and was about to clinch a fifth successive championship. 'That was some team,' Dorigo says. 'They had ten of the 11 from the Italian national side, and this was a time when there were no subs, so that was the national side.

'I wished I'd gone earlier in my career, but I liked it.' His family links to Italy and a desire to learn more, even in the latter stage of his career, made it an enjoyable break from Leeds. They still talked about John Charles in Turin too, just to make him feel a little more at home.

But, as Ian Rush so memorably pointed out, Italy was like a different country. 'You learn the darker things,' Dorigo says. 'I remember a game where a guy went down in a heap when I'd done nothing. I admit it looked good. Then he did the same thing a bit later. I found it frustrating and started swearing a bit. That was when Pierluigi Collina came charging over, those eyes bulging, blood vessels straining, and said, "I speak English perfectly. Don't do it again." I never did.

'They had a different mentality. If they went 2-0 down they would retreat and think better to lose 2-0 than 3-0, where I' was thinking, "We can get this back." In training they all needed to be told exactly what to do in every possible situation by the manager. If the manager didn't tell them they would look at each other and think, "What does he want me to do?" In England it was all a bit more chest-thumping, character-building stuff, but Italians wanted the tiny details.'

Dorigo played for Derby and Stoke too before retiring, but it is nice to see him back in Leeds, the city that named him the best player in the best season for almost half a century. He has the same gongs from Villa, Chelsea and Torino. Only Terry Cooper, with his white boots and Revie rose tint, could come close to him when working out the best player Leeds have ever had in that position. He put glamour into full-back play and, despite how he made it look, that is no easy thing.

8

Eddie Gray joined Leeds in 1963 and has never really left. Don Revie said that with any sort of luck he would have been bigger than George Best, but it is his resilience, niceness and forgiveness that have enhanced the legend. This examination, with Eddie's help, of just what he faced when he took over Leeds in 1982 – after relegation, and with the hooligan problem threatening the very existence of the club – shows how he provided shafts of optimism during the darkest times.

EDDIE GRAY: THE BEST FRIEND
LEEDS EVER HAD

BY ROB BAGCHI

'That wasn't a good part of the job,' says Eddie Gray with characteristic understatement, his first instinct, as ever, to protect the club he loves. Leeds United's most graceful player is talking about his debut season in management when the board sacked Allan Clarke following relegation after an 18-year spell in the First Division and persuaded Gray to become their first player-manager since Don Revie. 'It was pretty horrendous,' he continues. 'I can't say I enjoyed that side of it. It was a bad time for our football club but it wasn't just Leeds, it was generally in the game, and the club got over that.'

Unusually for the last two dozen Leeds managers, it is not a financial crisis Gray is citing as the principal impediment he faced when he took over in the summer of 1982 (though he was as strapped as the most beggarly of his successors). It was the escalating, debilitating consequences of recurrent outbreaks of violence in the stands and streets surrounding the Hawthorns, Blundell Park, the Baseball Ground et al that imperilled the club's very survival.

Apocalyptic warnings were commonplace at Elland Road from 2003 to 2007 and the more resilient among us became immune to the hysteria they aroused. At first, when the money ran out, the existential threats were so incessant that Sky Sports' Bryn Law would have been better off living in a caravan on Gelderd Road than going home at night, and the very sight of him provoked palpitations. Later, as a safeguard to sanity, we had either to adopt bemusement, develop a numbness to it or, better still, attempt to evolve a practical solution, working towards the day when Leeds United could be saved from the need for saviours once and for all.

But even during those turbulent days, as successive regimes either tried to put on a brave face or bluster their way through crises, never was an alarm issued as stark as the one the club published on the front of the programme for the Charlton Athletic match in November 1982. 'The future of Leeds United Association Football Club hangs in the balance,' read the statement in eye-boggling yellow script on a royal blue background, in place of a photograph on the cover. 'This in no way exaggerates the position and must not be taken as an idle threat. Despite repeated pleas and warnings, the mindless actions of a minority of the club's so-called followers last Saturday have placed an enormous degree of uncertainty over this great club. We would ask for the help and co-operation of everyone who has Leeds United at heart – and we appreciate that this is the majority of our supporters – to help rid the club of the "scab" element who, although small in numbers, have caused the club so many problems and whose loathsome actions now place the very existence of Leeds United in jeopardy.'

The appeal was made in sensational language, targeting the 'enemy within', and specifically referred to the victory over Newcastle United the Saturday before. Kevin Keegan had scored twice for Southampton on his last visit in April and his typically effervescent performance in that 3-1 defeat had shunted Leeds ever closer to relegation. In November, now in the monochrome stripes of his father's boyhood club, he paid the price when he and John Anderson were felled by missiles, one thrown from the Kop, the other from the Newcastle fans. Play was suspended for five minutes in the first-half and later seats were smashed and the debris lobbed over the south-east corner wasteland, raining down on pedestrians and those escaping the mêlée.

Yet only the location of the ominous notice and its loaded use of 'scabs' were extraordinary in a tempestuous few months for Leeds. Each of the six league and Cup home programmes before the Charlton game had included a mandatory reminder to the club's fans that, in the words of Ted Croker, the secretary of the Football Association, 'something had to be done and will be done' to tame what the tabloids called the 'scourge of hooliganism'. It was one of the stipulations the governing body insisted upon after it failed to nail Leeds for the conduct of their supporters on the night they effectively went down in May.

Towards the end of that 2-0 defeat by West Bromwich Albion, some of the 4,000 Leeds United fans in the Smethwick End managed to work the bolts free on the nine-foot fence caging them in, toppled it and then attempted to get on the pitch to halt the game. Three mounted policeman stopped the invasion and then 100 more officers were sent on a baton charge up the terrace to disperse everyone on to the streets. West Midlands police reported 34 injuries to their own side, 13 supporters hurt and made 36 arrests. One resident in splendid Cosmo Smallpiece specs appeared on the local teatime news the following day to report: 'They picked up bricks and that and bombarded the windows. I said, "Let's get the kiddies and let's get out." It was terrible.'

Clarke, gamely, said that he hadn't seen any trouble and endorsed 'our fans' as 'the best in the country'. It was a smart piece of work as far as his currency with the crowd was concerned, but the board had heard enough. He had begun 1982 falling short when trying to pull off an audacious coup by signing Peru's number 10, Julio Uribe, and arrived at its midpoint out of work. By the time a Falkland Island farmer, whose wireless had been confiscated at the beginning of April, used his first question after being liberated to ask a paratrooper 'have Leeds United been relegated?' the club were back in the Second Division, their followers routinely portrayed as savage scumbags, and the youngest of Revie's immortals was settling into the Don's chair.

The image of Eddie Gray that his name immediately invokes is a foolproof indicator of a Leeds fan's age. To some he will always be the sinuous dribbler of the late sixties and early seventies, Castlemilk-pale, Paul McCartney *Please Please Me* haircut, 'The Last Waltz', our George Best. My generation tends to conjure up visions of him after his comeback from the thigh injury in January 1975 that had seemingly ended his career: the gap between the digits on the 11 on his shirt now more widely spaced on a broader back, coathanger shoulders, the arms more prone to arc out like a vampire flapping his cape to shield the ball, socks slung so low you couldn't tell he was wearing any from the other side of the pitch, tongue protruding upwards as he lined up a sucker to con with a shimmy or a shake, still a magnificent footballer. Others will see him as the rookie manager, bright-eyed in his fag-ash grey Austin Reed suits and skinny ties, while those who encountered him a decade on will picture him in his club tracksuit, a man who treasured his great fortune to spend his working life in the fresh air, back where he belonged as mentor to Jonathan Woodgate, Stephen McPhail, Harry Kewell, Alan Smith and Matthew Jones. Youngsters will recognise him for his media work or his ambassadorial role, an astoundingly boyish-looking elder statesman whose passion and concern for the club is undiminished, the best friend Leeds United have ever had.

In 1982, at the age of 34, he was not the obvious choice for the job, and the board, at first, discussed re-hiring Revie's assistant, Maurice Lindley, as general manager, as they sifted through their options. Gray had impressed some of the

directors when coaching the youth side while facing up to
probable retirement in 1974–75, until Jimmy Armfield coaxed
him back, yet he says, 'It would never have occurred to me to
apply. I wanted to carry on playing as long as I could.' He had
one significant advantage over everyone else, he humbly admits
– he was already on the payroll.

'They were already paying me £25,000 a year as a player,' he
says. 'And they only had to give me an extra £5,000 to take it
on as player-manager. It all happened pretty quickly before pre-
season started. I met Mr Cussins and we came to an agreement
that we would give it a go. I didn't do it out of a sense of duty,
not at all. I'd been at the club a long, long time and I felt I
knew the club and how it ran. It wasn't a hard decision. In a
way, when I look back, maybe I should have just played on a
bit longer. I think if I hadn't become player-manager, and then
manager, and gone into that side I would have played on until
I was 40. From that point of view I may have done it a little bit
early. But I don't regret it.'

None of the five men who followed Revie had such
a threadbare legacy. Not only was the club in the Second
Division but it was lumbered with a fractured dressing room: a
split between Paul Hart and Kenny Burns, and one sundering
Trevor Cherry and Kevin Hird – not so much a back-four as
a quarrelling quartet. There were no transfer funds, a towering
wage bill and, though average crowds had risen by 3.4 per
cent to 22,109 as fans rallied to the cause during the battle
against relegation, they had fallen by 27 per cent during the
two exasperatingly sterile Jimmy Adamson years, and no one
expected anything other than another drastic decline.

As Gray prepared for the new season as favourites for
promotion, he took on an unbalanced squad with scope only to
demolish rather than repair or rebuild. The club was £2 million
in debt and he remembers the Inland Revenue appropriating

club cars in lieu of unpaid tax. Clarke had completed the retained list in the days between relegation and his dismissal, cutting adrift one high earner, Brian Greenhoff, who promptly set off on a Gleneagles Agreement-busting rebel tour of South Africa with a side put together by Jimmy Hill, Dennis Roach and the man the journalist Edward Pearce disdainfully collared as 'the member for Bloemfontein West', John Carlisle MP. With Greenhoff's £450-a-week basic salary off the books, Gray set about shedding as many of the other high earners as he could.

'We had a lot of players on good contracts that we couldn't really afford,' he says. 'And so one by one you had to try to move them on. Nothing detrimental to their playing abilities, the club just couldn't afford to keep them. It's tricky balancing it. You try to bring young players in through the system, and in the early days you introduce one or two, but you need the experienced players to help them along or the club could have fallen right through that division as well.'

Peter Barnes was the first to go, sent out on loan to Real Betis; then Derek Parlane left for Hong Kong. Frank Worthington stayed until December; Brian Flynn and Cherry lasted until midwinter; but Hart, who had been determined to leave in the summer, played out the last season on his contract. Burns confounded desultory expectations so well in only 19 appearances that he was named player of the year. David Seaman brought in £4,000 from Peterborough United, but had Gray known that John Lukic would ask for a transfer and be sold to Arsenal at the end of the season he would have made a different decision over which of his young goalies to keep.

While the economies were welcome, Leeds could not scrape together the £65,000 required to turn Neil McNab's loan from Brighton into a proper transfer and had to sacrifice their most popular player, Terry Connor, with 11 games to go (to introduce some variety into the attack) in a swap deal with Brighton for Andy Ritchie.

'Neil was very impressed and happy during his stay at Elland Road and I think he would have been happy to stay there, had the financial aspect been sorted out satisfactorily,' Ritchie said on signing. 'After I'd flown up to see Eddie Gray I could see why. He has a marvellous knack of getting on with people and he communicates with players. That's half the battle of being a successful manager.'

At that stage Leeds had recovered on the field from a dip and fought back to fifth with an impressive run in March that took them to seven points off a promotion place with 11 games to play after Easter. They had begun with only one defeat from their first 12 games, using Cherry effectively as a spare man at the back with Gray himself and Hird as wing-backs. Slowly, they established themselves as contenders until the departures of Worthington and Cherry took a temporary toll. Five draws and two defeats from their final seven games ruined their chances and they faded to eighth in this pre-play-off era, ten points behind Leicester in third.

Financially the club was being reconfigured, constricting budgets were enforced and the first shoots of Bill Fotherby's commercial revolution since joining the board in 1981 were beginning to bear promise. In March Gray was able to make his first cash signing, a staggered deal worth £85,000 to Dumbarton for John Donnelly, a left-sided attack-minded midfielder. Gray may have seen something of himself in Donnelly's courage and confidence on the ball, but the younger Glaswegian shared none of his manager's dedication. Gray encouraged his players to enjoy playing for Leeds and explicitly told them to express themselves. Donnelly did this best in the bars and clubs of the city. When upbraided by the young manager for drinking on a Friday before a game, Donnelly protested, 'But I only had six pints.' Gray, supposedly the 'choirboy' of Revie's Leeds, could be excused a few expletives, although an unreliable signing was a piddling problem compared with his other burdens.

On the terraces Leeds remained in serious bother. A fortnight before Gray's first season began the board escaped punishment for the Hawthorns riot because the FA had been unable to push through sanctions on Chelsea for failing to control their travelling supporters when threatened by legal action. Leeds, too, made the point that the club's fans away from Elland Road could not be their responsibility, and the FA was unwilling to test its contention in the High Court. Relief lasted barely a fortnight – the first game of the season took Leeds to Grimsby, where one Leeds fan ran onto the pitch and grabbed a ball out of the hands of a home player as he ran out of the tunnel; others caused extensive damage to the away stand; assaults around Cleethorpes preceded the game and resumed after it had finished in a 1-1 draw. Fifty-seven arrests were made.

Grimsby tried to withhold United's portion of the gate receipts but were eventually ordered to hand it over. Croker said, 'Leeds United can expect an in-depth investigation. The FA intends to take strong action against persistent misconduct.' The directors, trying to head it off, asked the 23 Second Division clubs to quadruple ticket prices when United hit town, but since so much of the trouble happened away from the ground it seems a preposterously myopic view of the phenomenon of hooliganism.

The FA's warning didn't quell the violence nor did the repeated urgings of Cussins and Gray. There were fights at Hillsborough in September, battery in Blackburn and a sequence of brawls before the game at Chelsea in October that spread out underground and overground from Piccadilly Circus to Charing Cross. After Keegan was struck by a coin on 30 October, the FA considered its response and ordered Leeds to close the terraces for the first two home matches in December, which then drew crowds of 11,528 and 8,741. Special magistrates' courts were set up in Barnsley before the match at Oakwell – shades of Judge Nutmeg – to deal with the scores of arrests and in the new year at Derby, £20,000 worth of damage was inflicted on the Baseball Ground.

Each time Gray, whose appointment *The Times*' Peter Ball called 'a masterstroke of public relations', was obliged to condemn the violence and appeal to the better natures of Leeds' supporters. 'We had the reputation,' he says, 'and you cannot deny there's a certain element of the football club then that never did the club any favours.' Indeed, so frequent were his appeals for calm and consideration that by September 1983 he was invited to address the Police Superintendents' Association conference in Torquay on the whole issue of hooliganism, the manager now an accidental expert. For all his injunctions for tolerance, his advice to the press not to glorify the 'war stories' of those involved and entreaties to ban sales of alcohol around grounds, it haunted his entire spell as manager.

There were multiple arrests at Portsmouth, Newcastle and Middlesbrough, and later on in his second season, when Chelsea won 5-0 at Stamford Bridge to seal promotion back to the First Division, some of the Leeds supporters demolished the scoreboard and took fragments of it back to Yorkshire on the train. Mounted police had to disperse those fighting on the pitch.

At the beginning of his third season Gray stopped his family from travelling to watch the team away from home after a volley of missiles were hurled from the Leeds end at Huddersfield, and he implored opponents to make their home games against Leeds all-ticket though some, willing to risk it for a pay day, refused.

Oxford, who sold tickets on the gate in November 1984, had to clear the Manor Ground of six-foot planks and scaffolding polls dismantled from a TV gantry at the top of which was a teetering cameraman who must have suffered the worst day of his life. These were lobbed onto the pitch by some Leeds fans and the periodic outbreaks of pandemonium were shown on *Match of the Day* where Gray said he had offered to concede the game ten minutes from the end rather than endanger the players further. Leeds lost 5-2.

The sense that the club had hit rock bottom was pervasive throughout the rest of the country, but the campaign ended with a riot at Birmingham City, during which Ian Hambridge, a 15-year-old boy from Northampton, suffered head injuries when a wall collapsed under the weight of fans fleeing a police baton charge and died in hospital the next day. Gray had been asked by a police officer to make an appeal when the violence began but found an audience too riled to listen. 'It had no effect whatsoever,' he says. 'I remember going down there to try to quieten them down and they were throwing bricks onto the pitch, which wasn't a nice thing. Times like that you feel like walking away from it.'

Looking back at it now, almost 35 years on, the density of disorder seems scarcely believable. Living through it as a teenager, though, was to exist without perspective. It did not seem normal, that would be too trite, but neither did it feel particularly exceptional. If we were the most hated club in the country then so be it; it only burnished our sense of grievance and deep suspicion of the FA and Football League. But for Gray it was torture and you could hear his distress when duty called and he had to rue what was being done to 'the good name of Leeds United'. If at times he felt helpless to stop the tide that was because he was. Yet it was he who kept kindling hope in the only way a football manager can – by demonstrating that he had a coherent long-term revival strategy based on sound principles that signalled a way back.

In his second season he spent the money raised by selling Parlane to Manchester City and Arthur Graham to Manchester United on two Scots, George McCluskey and Andy Watson who turned out to be too lightweight for the roles for which he had bought them – centre-forward and midfield ball-winner. McCluskey had a wonderful touch and would later show signs of his Parkhead class out wide, but he could not handle Second Division centre-halves continually kicking the crap out of him.

Some Leeds managers who had once been elegant players – Revie and George Graham especially – favoured footballers whose steely, ruthless qualities they themselves had lacked. Until late in his third season when he signed Ian Baird, Gray seemed to prefer ball-players like himself. Sadly, at the prices he was buying them at they would always be flawed, usually by a lack of physical presence, often a shortage of diligence, sometimes both.

Better, then, as Revie had done, to fashion your own, and fortunately for Gray he found one right under his nose in the reserve team, a first-year professional who was enjoying his second chance after being released by Manchester City. John Sheridan was 18, diffident around senior players, though relaxed around and esteemed by the younger residents of his digs – Tommy Wright, Scott Sellars and Denis Irwin. The manager hoped that he would 'come out of his shell' if moved up to train with the first-team squad, and quickly recognised that the Sheridan who crossed the white line was a far different animal from the bashful lad who tried to make himself as inconspicuous as possible in the changing rooms.

'John had a good knowledge of how to play the game,' says Gray. 'Most importantly, he never looked ruffled. He always had time and space. People think that's easy. It's not. It's knowledge – how to get in the game, how to bring other people into the game, and John played at the highest level. He was a top-class player. You could see that right away. He was as mentally tough as any 18-year-old I've ever worked with.

'When I first took over I'd heard about this boy. He was supposed to be pretty quiet and shy. He didn't particularly mix well at that particular time, and I took him on to train with the first team. As soon as I'd seen him he was never going back to the reserves again. I put him in our team as a very young player because he had the talent and ability. On the field, especially when he was younger, he felt he was as good as anybody. A touch of arrogance – that's part of the nature of the game. It's what you have to do. It doesn't come easy but it was just in John's makeup – he knew he could pass the ball, he knew how to get into the game, bring other people into the game. That was his gift.'

It was a hint of swagger that immediately caught the eye, and then you noticed the crisp, accurate passing, both long and short, and the precision matching his judgement of the best option for the team. He always played with his head up, scanning the field, and would even break stride to point players into space, part conductor, part traffic cop. That was the origin of the famous banner 'Sheridan Dictates' and he became an even better player under Billy Bremner, more open to employing his thunderous shooting power as he laboured tirelessly, often seemingly single-handedly, to drag Leeds out of the division.

Sheridan broke his leg at Barnsley two months into Gray's second season and with the player-manager struggling with back and hamstring injuries, and his younger brother Frank hobbled at Christmas, prospects for the project looked bleak. Wright, who had made his debut as a 17-year-old the season before, and Sellars, now 18, were brought in, the former as a foil to McCluskey, only to outstrip him as a goalscoring threat with his bullocking pace and self-assurance as a finisher. Sellars, blossoming under Gray's personal tuition, was a superb passer and slotted in on the left. That Bremner should prefer more robust, physically imposing players would persuade him to squander both of them.

In Sheridan's absence they became regulars, but four successive defeats in December had left United in 19th, four points and one spot above the relegation places. Seldom had the club been in a worse position. There was no money and there wouldn't be even after the board sold the ground to the council in 1985 for £2.5 million to clear the debts and directors' loans. The only fit player with any significant experience, David Harvey, had a beguiling rather than a commanding personality, the Scots were struggling as a whole and Gray's promising kids were in danger of being overwhelmed.

Imagine, therefore, the surprise of those of us who turned up for the home game against Middlesbrough on New Year's Eve to hear over the Tannoy that things had become so desperate that the manager had named a 37-year-old great on the bench, whose last appearance for the club more than five years previously had also coincided with Jock Stein's final match as manager. And yet convincing Peter Lorimer, who had been training with Leeds during Vancouver Whitecaps' winter break and was made unemployed when the NASL folded, to return was a masterstroke. 'All the boys looked up to him and got on well with him,' says Gray. 'It was a great benefit to the younger players when he came back.'

If, we joked, the man who had left us as '90 miles an hour' had reappeared looking like '90 pies', he did not play like a man hindered by a slight paunch. He wasn't the irrepressibly marauding presence of old, of course, but, remarkably, the 'hotshot' was as blistering as ever and he used his intelligence to organise the team, to keep spirits up if they lost a goal, and pick out opportunities with his masterly passing and vision.

With him back on the right of midfield, Leeds won eight of their next 11 games and finished the season safely in 10th.

'I'm helping to keep the young lads balanced,' Lorimer said of his role. 'If someone's being dragged out of position or rushing things, or whatever, I'll have a quiet word. You can't expect kids to notice, because they're concentrating on their own game.'

With Sheridan fit at the start of the next season, Leeds made a flying start with four successive victories and with Irwin, Neil Aspin and Andy Linighan joining Sellars and Wright as first-team regulars. At times they were scintillating – hammering Oldham 6-0, Notts County 5-0 and Wimbledon 5-2 in a match that seemed to capture all the verve of Gray's young side, crowned by Sellars' back-heel and drag-back tackle that set up an exquisite chip which diddled Dave Beasant. Yet they were undone by a maddening inconsistency away from home that was all part of their education.

After Baird joined just before the old March deadline day, they started to attack with more punch and beat Manchester City away and league leaders Oxford at home. Baird scored in those games, twice in the next, a 2-2 draw with Wimbledon, and the only goal in the 1-0 victory over Shrewsbury that meant they went to St Andrew's on the final day to play Birmingham City, who had already secured their return to the First Division, as one of five teams with a chance of grabbing the last promotion place. As we know, they lost on the club's darkest day, the other four won and Manchester City went up.

Five months later Leslie Silver, chairman since 1983, sacked Gray after 11 games of a league campaign that had begun badly before a five-match unbeaten run had steadied a listing ship. The season before had illustrated their potential but the road to fulfilment is tortuous for a team with so many young players – a side that now had 17-year-old Terry Phelan at left-back. 'A lot of the boys went on to have great careers,' says Gray, of whom they all continue to speak with great respect and affection. 'I felt that when the club let me go things were just beginning to happen. The players were getting stronger, but I can understand from the club's point of view that they were impatient, they wanted things to happen quicker, and you have to accept the consequences. That's the nature of football and you accept it. People who run football clubs make the decisions and you've got to abide by them. You don't necessarily agree with them.'

The remarkable thing is that nobody did. Rare are the times a club fires its manager and condemnation is universal. There were protests at Elland Road, Gray's distraught players threatened to go on strike, and there was a general sense that a dreadful mistake had been made. Without the money to compete, Gray had followed Revie's example and tried to generate something sustainable through nurturing the talent developed by the youth team and one or two astute, cheap purchases. Where Revie had Bobby Collins, Gray had Lorimer, but he was unable to buy international players of the calibre of Johnny Giles and Alan Peacock, without whom promotion might never have come in 1964.

It was a lost opportunity and Bremner gutted the side in pursuit of a more direct, pragmatic approach. Phelan was released and went on to win the FA Cup with Wimbledon; Linighan won the title and scored the winning goal in an FA Cup final for Arsenal; Ian Snodin won the First Division with Everton; Sellars cost Howard Wilkinson £1 million when he brought him back in 1992; Irwin won the treble at Manchester United (among seven Premier League championships); and Sheridan joined Irwin and Phelan in the Republic of Ireland side at the 1994 World Cup. All of them owed their starts in the game to Eddie Gray. And Leeds United owe him recognition for keeping his head in those rough, riotous seasons to keep the beacon burning, the most important work he ever did for the club in 55 years of immaculate service.

9

John Charles once explained how he had signed for Juventus despite never having heard of them, and how he saved Omar Sívori, the 1961 European footballer of the year, from a Mafia bullet. The Argentinian had been threatened with sudden death if he scored in a particular game. Almost inevitably, a ball ricocheted off the back of his head and into the goal. Charles and his teammates formed a protective cortège around Sivori and shuffled down the tunnel. Charles then scored the winner, but it was disallowed. He asked the referee why. 'Like Mr Sívori, I want to get home safely,' he said. He was more than just a great raconteur and scored 157 goals in 327 appearances in two spells at Leeds (1947–57 and 1962), despite being just at home up front or in defence. He was a softly spoken hero, although Jack Charlton took issue with the 'Gentle Giant' moniker. 'When he went on a surge he would leave a terrible trail of human devastation in his wake,' he said. 'Bloody gentle giant indeed!'

JOHN CHARLES: WHAT COULD HAVE BEEN, AND WHAT WAS

BY ROBERT ENDEACOTT

This is the story of three Leeds United men, three united men with differing degrees of prominence in the football history books. But all important. One became world famous, the other two nowhere near, though they did play significant parts in the epic Leeds United story. Regardless of your age, John Charles you will almost certainly know of, the other two perhaps not, but stay and read this ramble along the misty walkways of nostalgia and that will all change.

John Charles was born in Swansea in December 1931, a few years before the other two young men of this unlikely trio, John Reynolds and Peter McConnell. Reynolds was born in Neath in November 1936, while McConnell was born in Reddish near Stockport, the following March. Unless you were there to experience life during and after the Second World War it is difficult to imagine how people in this country coped with the effects of so much destruction, loss and hardship. There is a sense that youngsters of the era, like Charles, Reynolds and McConnell, grew up with more personal pressures and responsibilities than future generations yet became more resilient, pragmatic and independent as a result. Precious few privileges were given to children of those times, everything had to be earned – as well as food being rationed, sweets were a rarity, and even access to a football was a luxury for many.

Selected by manager Major Frank Buckley (a 'proper character' in his own right), John Charles' league debut came in April 1949, near the end of the 1948–49 season. It had been another bland season in Division Two for the team, Leeds having never shown themselves as serious contenders for promotion. Relegation had also looked unlikely, though things came too close for comfort in the later weeks of the campaign. They eventually came 15th in the table out of 22 teams. With two points for a win and one for a draw, two teams going up and two going down, Leeds finished with just two more points than second-bottom Nottingham Forest.

By then yet to turn 18, Charles' debut made him the youngest ever player to appear for the club. (His great friend of the future, Peter Lorimer, would break that record and hold it for many years.) Charles played in defence against Blackburn Rovers, at centre-half, in what was in effect a back line of five: two full-backs, a right-half and a left-half to each side of the 'big lad' in the middle. He performed well in the 0-0 draw. A few days before, Leeds had played a midweek friendly against Queen of the South and Charles had played centre-half then too. He was directly up against Billy 'Basher' Houliston, a formidable centre-forward (his nickname provides an idea of his playing style) who represented Scotland on three occasions, including a famous 3-1 victory over mighty England at Wembley just two weeks prior to the friendly. The Leeds v Queen of the South tie ended as a stalemate and, after the match, Houliston praised Charles, describing him as one of the best centre-halves he had ever played against.

The following season saw Charles as an ever-present in the old gold shirts (with blue sleeves) of Leeds. He would also be capped by Wales, becoming the youngest ever player to represent the country, though his debut was a personally disappointing affair and it would be a while before he was called up again. Regardless, Leeds vastly improved with him in the team, lifting their standings in both the league and the

FA Cup. They finished 5th in Division Two, five points behind the next three teams and nine off first-placed Spurs, with Sheffield Wednesday also winning promotion as runners-up. Leeds reached the quarter-finals of the FA Cup, narrowly losing 1-0 away to Arsenal, who went on to win the competition against Liverpool in the Wembley final. It is no coincidence that the 'birth' of John Charles as a first-team regular saw that upturn in Leeds' fortunes, but he wasn't the type of person to let success go to his head or to brag about it. Not that his teammates would ever allow the 'whippersnapper' to get too big for his boots anyway. He was still just a young lad to them, albeit a supremely talented one.

Outstanding at most sports he ever participated in, at school his teachers fought a long and losing battle in trying to educate him academically. Charles just wanted to play football, and that was that. Younger brother Mel displayed exactly the same attitude a few years later. A predictable and obvious consequence of disinterest in John's studies was a lack of qualifications when he left school to join the 'adult world' aged 15. Thankfully, along with a batch of other hopeful football players, he was taken on by Swansea Town as a junior member of their ground staff. This was a bright development for him as his career options were extremely limited due to his academic underachievement. In Swansea, by far the likeliest work destination for boys was the coalmine. As football clubs weren't allowed to sign players on professional terms until they had reached the age of 17, this ground-staff route into their employment was commonplace. It's exactly how John Reynolds and Peter McConnell also found their way to Elland Road nearly five years later.

Unfortunately for Charles and the other 15 year-olds at Swansea Town, the matter of playing football matches was not high on their employers' work rota. To add to that disappointment, Charles received little encouragement from the staff and suspected he was never going to be given a fair chance to prove himself. Even though it beat working down the pit – a fact he would never, of course, forget – he felt unwanted and disregarded and, despite his great enthusiasm to learn as much about football as he could, no one seemed interested in teaching him.

This wasn't actually the case but by the time Swansea realised their perceived neglect Leeds had already 'wooed' Charles right from under their noses, so to speak, thanks to the efforts of their chief scout for South Wales, the influential and persuasive Jack Pickard. He had watched Charles in training sessions and was excited by his potential, envisioning a bright future for him, providing he received the quality training fashioned to suit his specific needs. There was an excellent football player within him and it was the duty of coaching staff to bring it out. Major Buckley and his staff at Elland Road were capable of doing that. Pickard visited the Charles household and told them that while Leeds United were not one of the 'big boys' in the Football League (yet) they were ambitious, possessed great potential, just like John, and they were wealthier than Swansea and knew how to properly treat their footballers.

Charles made what was a brave decision to leave his roots to gauge for himself what life in Leeds would be like. And though he had the support of his loving family to bolster him as he took the long journey up to the West Riding, it really is true that his mum said he couldn't go to England because he didn't own a passport. Initially, for a few weeks, he was a triallist until Major Buckley, agreeing with Jack Pickard's judgement, decided he had seen enough in the young man to warrant offering him a full-time contract.

It may come as a surprise but, in life away from football, John Charles was terribly shy. Not modest but actually shy, never comfortable being the centre of attention. And, for a man who loved playing in front of huge crowds, he disliked being part of a crowd. As his career blossomed with Leeds he gained more and more fans around the country and was forever flattered by praise and adulation. Not that he ever really understood it. After all, he was only kicking and heading a football about. To be paid for that simply made him feel like one of the luckiest people alive. He felt there was nothing special about him. He was no big-head. He knew his place and therefore wasn't swayed by all the praise. That isn't to say he didn't rate himself as a footballer, because he did. He knew exactly how good he was and he knew he could get better. Typical of the man, though, he was forever quick to recognise and give credit to all the coaches, managers and fellow players who helped him succeed.

In spite of his imposing height and build, he was against throwing his weight around to intimidate or harm opponents. To do so, he believed, would signify a loss of self-control which in turn would detract from the quality of his own performance. Such mild-mannered behaviour annoyed teammates throughout his entire career, but he stayed the same as, he insisted, violence was never the answer – there were always better solutions. Certain teammates called him soft, others argued that his placid attitude merely encouraged the 'roughneck' opponents to try to batter him and goad him even more. Charles would learn later in his career – and his patience would be tested much more heavily too – that it was actually a higher class of thuggery in British football, but he disliked bullies in any circumstance.

Charles would always try to see good in people. Those who tried their hardest in life earned his admiration too, regardless of their personal backgrounds. With a playful sense of humour, he rarely objected to being the butt of the joke – which was a good thing, as his great pal Harold Williams was often a rascal whenever his compatriot was around – and he knew that he wasn't the quickest-witted when it came to returning the jokes and pranks anyway.

The 1950–51 campaign signified another strong effort from Leeds, but one which ultimately proved fruitless again. A strong finish to the season had been ruined by a poor start and they had never been in the running for the top two places. For the second consecutive season they finished fifth in Division Two, and promotion to Division One remained just a hope. Charles played in defence for the majority of the season until late March when an injury crisis struck Leeds' attacking options. And so, surprisingly, Major Buckley selected Charles as centre-forward for the match at Manchester City. Leeds were soundly beaten and Charles hardly got a look-in. Nonetheless, two days later, versus Hull City, he again played up front and this time everything seemed to go right as he scored twice in the 3-0 win.

Charles didn't know what to think. Playing as centre-forward was new to him and he felt awkward, but after the match Buckley put him in the picture, saying, 'Well done, lad. You'll stay at centre-forward.'

Aged 18 in 1950, life got more complicated as he was called away on compulsory National Service along with thousands of others. National Service ('peacetime conscription') was a consequence of World War Two and would continue to be enforced until 1960. Charles would be stationed with the 12th Royal Lancers based in Carlisle, Cumbria, a place not too inconvenient in terms of distance, even taking into account the absence of any motorways at the time. This did not prevent him from making regular appearances for Leeds as, like other professional football players in similar circumstances, he was often granted special dispensation to play for his side.

Tommy Taylor of Manchester United was stationed with Charles and they played in the same army team. The arrangement indirectly came with a price: the army made sure that Charles played for them too, and in 1952 he captained the Lancers' side to win the Army Cup, no mean feat. Had he had his way he would have played sports all day long anyway as it was much better 'work' than repainting military vehicles and equipment. He also represented the Lancers at boxing, winning all of his bouts and prompting popular opinion that he would easily make it as a professional boxer. Except there was the rather large problem, to the consternation and irritation of his already irate army sergeants, of Charles not wanting to box due to his hatred of inflicting pain on anyone. Boxing did help certain aspects of his game, though, including discipline and self-control, plus stamina, balance and physical reflexes.

During his time at Carlisle Charles underwent cartilage operations on his knees, causing him to miss over half of Leeds' games in the 1951–52 season. He had often felt discomfort in his knees before joining the army, so the procedures probably came at a good time, in that he was under the army's care and not the football club's when they were performed. He was able to return to the Leeds side that winter and Major Buckley restored him to the centre of defence.

The following spring Leeds trialled dozens more hopeful lads looking to earn the chance of a career in football. The 15-year-olds who sufficiently impressed the Leeds staff would then be offered terms to work as apprentice ground staff-cum-trainee players until they were 17, the earliest age at which football clubs could take them on full-time.

Two of the successful triallists were John Reynolds and Peter McConnell. Reynolds, in particular, impressed and was anticipated, even at such an early stage, to develop into a special talent, be that as a defender or as a striker. He was quick, strong, good with both feet and even taller than Charles had been at the same age, suggesting that he also would be exceptional in the air. A general view was that he needed to gain more muscle, but that would easily happen if John Charles' situation was anything to go by, flourishing from a gangly youth into a strapping young man in the space of just a few months.

Although not as eye-catching as John Reynolds, Peter McConnell also looked to be a useful and promising prospect. For as long as he could remember, he had wanted to play inside-right. The Elland Road staff, however, considered him better suited to the more defensive role of right-half. Like his mate, he was strong, quick and good with both feet, and he was an exceptional tackler with a never-give-in attitude. He was one of those lads who would help the cause in whichever way was thought best, and when it came to football he was willing to play in any position as long as he got a game (with the exception of keeper – he considered all goalkeepers to be a little bit insane).

As they both came from South Wales, John Reynolds had, of course, heard of John Charles, but they were not acquainted. That changed once their Leeds United connection was forged and they soon became good friends, at times travelling from Leeds to Swansea and back together by rail. In fact, as the journey often involved overnight travel on a GPO mail train with no sleeper carriage – which they wouldn't have wanted to pay for anyway – one of them would stretch out in a compartment on the single-cushioned bench, the other on the overhead luggage rack. The cushioned bench was always the preferred 'bed' and so the two Johns would toss a coin for the privilege, as Charles wasn't the sort to pull rank on a friend. Oddly enough though, the younger Reynolds never seemed to win that particular contest.

It was not long before some of the youngsters would be 'promoted' to training with the first-team players. McConnell got on well with Charles too, and many a time the Welshman would ask him to pop across Elland Road to the newsagent's to get him cigarettes or football coupons. Discreetly, of course.

Less discreet orders given to McConnell often came from trainer/ coach Bob Roxburgh on the Fullerton Park training pitches on mornings when Charles was late for training. Being Leeds' star player had little bearing on his attitude to training, which was deplorable. When he finally did arrive to join his teammates (he lived 200 hundred or so yards away from the stadium) he was still usually the last to complete the drills, runs and races. Roxburgh's patience was always tested when it came to Charles' punctuality, and this commonly resulted in him telling McConnell to 'Go and get the lazy bastard out of his bed!'

Like all the recruits of the same arrival year, McConnell and Reynolds worked hard, trained hard, listened hard and, in matches, played hard. Both had been brought up with the doctrine that to succeed in anything they had to try their very best. While the Leeds seniors, the first team, continued to frustrate everyone, the lads' team, Leeds' youth or junior side, gelled well and made strong progress in all competitions such as the league, the FA Youth Cup and even overseas tournaments. In the 1953–54 season, thanks to notable victories over Blackburn Rovers, Blackpool, Bury, and then a very strong Manchester City side, the Leeds youngsters were drawn to play West Bromwich Albion away in the fifth round of the FA Youth Cup. In that side of good players Peter McConnell and John Reynolds were the shining lights. Indeed, in Reynolds' case, he showed so much promise that there were predictions that he could well be 'the next John Charles'.

All that changed on Tuesday 1 September at the Hawthorns ground. Playing as centre-forward Reynolds tussled for the ball but his leg buckled beneath him due to excessive pressure, and his knee ligaments were severely damaged. He would be out injured for a long time, even missing the replay which did not take place for five months. West Bromwich won it.

National Service also proved an obstacle on the pair's career path in early 1955 when they had turned 18. Because of the long recovery process for his damaged knee Reynolds was put on light duties by the army. For a time both he and Peter McConnell were stationed at Catterick in North Yorkshire, though McConnell also spent time in Germany. As neither of them was a first-team regular for Leeds they were not granted any special dispensations, though they did manage to attend some Leeds home matches as enthusiastic spectators. The side was most assuredly on the up by then, and John Charles' reputation was spreading fast, as both a defender and as an attacker. Raich Carter had replaced Major Buckley as United manager by this time, and early in the 1954–55 campaign the new boss was compelled to restore Charles to the back line due to a run of five consecutive defeats in their first six matches.

Carter was not a particularly popular appointment – in fact, he was one of the very few people in life Charles never got on with – but the team undoubtedly improved and steadily climbed the table. A fine player in his time, Carter's man-management skills left a lot to be desired. In April 1955 Leeds finished fourth, missing out on promotion to Division One by a solitary point. Third-placed Rotherham United suffered even more, losing out due to inferior goal average compared to Birmingham City and Luton Town above them on the same number of points – 54.

But the tide had turned. The following season, after nine seemingly interminable years, Leeds won promotion to the top division, finishing the campaign in second place as runners-up to champions Sheffield Wednesday. It was a memorable season for John Charles too, scoring 29 goals in 41 league games.

Leeds' return to Division One proved to be exciting, dramatic, memorable and pride-restoring. Unlikely as it might have seemed then, at times the team actually flirted with the top spot, and by the close John Charles had scored an astonishing

38 goals in 40 league appearances, although the team's form had dipped in the second half of the season and they eventually finished in eighth place.

Off the field, serious events occurred in September 1956 to actually threaten the club's existence, though the gravity of the situation was not so obvious at first. During the early hours of Tuesday 18 September a fire raged through the West Stand of Elland Road destroying virtually everything in its reach. Luckily, no lives were lost, not even the unofficial club cat Blackie, who had gone missing at the time of the blaze but returned a few days later, hungry and bemused. However, the fire had been so ferocious that large sections of the pitch were scorched by the heat and the stand was left looking like the charred skeleton of a huge whale, according to press reports of the era. The flames had enveloped the whole structure and everything within it, including the offices, football kits, club records, physiotherapy equipment, dressing rooms, directors' rooms and press box.

The fire was disastrous to Leeds United's finances, particularly because the insurance cover fell way short of the costs needed to pay for a suitable replacement to be designed and built. Chairman Sam Bolton insisted that the club did not want to sell John Charles, their main asset, and that they would do their utmost to keep him: 'If we'd sold John eighteen months ago we would not be in Division One. It's all right saying "sell John to buy a stand", but I'd rather keep our good players and have a stand comparable with the old one than sell to make a better ground. Why should Leeds United rear footballers to sell to other people?'

Alas, as time wore on, it became clear that they had no option but to sell their most prized player. Chairman Bolton at least had enough influence to insist they would not sell Charles to any clubs in the English Football League. This did help ease the burden of losing him for many Leeds fans who, to their credit, generally understood and sympathised with the club and the predicament caused by the fire. Juventus of Turin were the highest bidders, paying a record fee for a British player of £65,000. John and Peggy Charles were keen on the move to a new country – a new world, really – taking their three young sons (Terry, Melvyn and baby Peter) with them to embark on their new adventure. The income from the club's reluctant sale of the man who would become 'Il Gigante Buono' (loose translation: 'the Gentle Giant') to his adoring Italian fans, arguably kept them in business; Charles' transfer might well have saved them. John Charles left Leeds but Leeds never left John Charles, and he would be back.

After their conscripted stints in the army, Peter McConnell and John Reynolds returned to their place of civilian work in 1957. Leeds United now had a new main stand but no 'main' player, no John Charles. And, sadly, there would be no John Reynolds to feature in a Leeds United first team either. His general fitness was good but the knee injury could not mend sufficiently, crucially and painfully failing him in many attempted playing comebacks.

Peter McConnell's playing career progressed slowly but surely, and he made his Leeds United first-team debut on 20 December 1958, versus Bolton Wanderers at Elland Road. This was just over three weeks since Leeds had signed Don Revie from Sunderland. The visitors won 4-3, helped by a hat-trick scored by Bolton's famed centre-forward, 'the Lion of Vienna', Nat Lofthouse. McConnell played as wing-half and performed reasonably well, certainly not embarrassing himself. He went on to play just five more first-team games that season though, with Leeds finishing 15th in the table, and played eight times in the next campaign, where Leeds finished an abysmal 21st and were relegated back to Division Two.

The 1960–61 season was a shock to the system for the team: no quick return to the top division here, not a chance of it – instead, a let-down of large proportions as they finished the season in an unimpressive position of 14th. It could have been much worse: another relegation had been a genuine possibility.

Matters came to a head when manager Jack Taylor departed and, after a short while, in March 1961, a surprise name was announced as his replacement. Don Revie would be the new Leeds player-manager. This development probably surprised Revie himself. It certainly surprised Peter McConnell because, after one match in which both men appeared, Revie had confided in McConnell that he had been offered the job as player-manager for another club, Bournemouth and Boscombe. Not only that but he wanted to take McConnell with him to captain the south-coast outfit.

Everyone knows that Revie's management helped the team narrowly avoid the dreaded drop that season, and that he was highly appreciative of McConnell's steadfast efforts on the pitch. McConnell wasn't a flair player. He had little flamboyance about him, but few players could match his commitment and passion for the cause at a time when it was desperately needed by Revie's Leeds side.

That need had dissipated by the start of the following season, Revie's first full campaign as boss. He had been generously funded by the club but, as they were heavily in debt, he had to manage his transfer budget very carefully. In other words, he needed to use the marketplace astutely, and this involved selling players as well as buying them. He didn't want to lose McConnell but, as he told the player, he had to make sacrifices, and as he had received a decent offer for him, he was willing, reluctantly, to let McConnell leave Leeds.

McConnell appreciated Revie's candour and so decided to listen to what his prospective new employers had to offer.

Carlisle United's manager Ivor Powell had been hoping to sign him for a good while and his wishes were finally realised as McConnell agreed to the deal. He went on to enjoy an outstanding career there and became one of the fans' most popular players.

John Reynold's playing career was mercilessly cut short by injury but the club were supportive and treated him well, taking him on full-time on the ground staff, where his work involved reporting to head groundsman Cec Burroughs, another great Leeds servant. Very much in line with the 'Keep Fighting' sign on the wall of the first-team dressing room (placed there by short-term manager Bill Lambton, another unpopular boss) John Reynolds kept on battling and eventually reached the top of his game for the club, off the field of play, as head groundsman. He would become a genuine and good friend to countless people across the history of Leeds United.

Were he a 26 year-old player in today's game, what would John Charles be worth in the transfer market? Nat Lofthouse and Billy Wright were recognised as two England greats of the 1950s. Lofthouse was once asked who the best centre-half he had played against was, and he answered, 'John Charles.' Wright was asked who the greatest centre-forward he had faced was, and he too named John Charles. It is safe to guess that Charles would be worth around the same as, say, Wembley Stadium, were the national institution and landmark ever to be put up for sale – which, of course, is a ludicrous thought, isn't it?

Do present-day Leeds United need a new world great remotely as good as John Charles? Well, it would be brilliant if we ever see one again but, in my humble opinion, I see Leeds as more in need of other particular qualities first, as exemplified by not only John Charles but the unsung Peter McConnell and John Reynolds too.

John Charles died in 2004 and, of course, many thousands mourned. John Reynolds died in 2012, but he stands as a fabulous example of the true camaraderie a club needs to thrive, and he exemplified the spirit of family and community which Don Revie rebuilt the club around, transforming it into a world-class force.

Peter McConnell still lives in his beloved Leeds, where he suffers from a painful lower-back condition brought on, he jokes, by having to carry a certain Billy Bremner through the flame-haired Scotsman's early games for Leeds United.

10

What happens when you make it? **Noel Whelan** was a Premier League player at 18 and thought it would last for ever. Here he fights Carlton Palmer, gets chased through the streets by Phil Masinga, and reveals the scale of Arsenal sledging. After only 48 games it was over, and he still feels the pain now as he recalls the tears he shed after that Sunday-morning call from Howard Wilkinson. If anyone questions the passion of the pro player then they should read this. It hurts.

NOEL WHELAN, PART TWO: SNOWY

BY ADAM POPE

'I made my debut for Leeds United away to Sheffield Wednesday at Hillsborough in May 1993 at the age of 19. I'd been in and out of the reserve side, so I was pretty much playing two or three games a week with the players who weren't actually in the first team. We had an abundance of midfield talent: David Rocastle, Scott Sellars, Gary McAllister, Gordon Strachan, David Batty, Gary Speed and Steve Hodge. That reserve side was ridiculous, absolutely ridiculous, when you look at some of the big names there who were England internationals. It was so strong. So, for us playing with those sorts of players, it was great experience in learning the trade and getting better.

'Finally, after feeling I'd been on the fringes for a while, I got the call-up. The manager Howard Wilkinson liked me but he put a lot of pressure on me. He worked me hard off the pitch, in and around the ground. He was pushing and driving me and I felt he was picking on me at times. But I now know it was to instil more discipline because I had a bit of attitude, a bit of arrogance and a swagger. They used to call it "the Whelan swagger" when I would come in with my bow-legs, strolling across the field with that innate confidence. You know, you've got to have that.

'The confidence came out again when I got chosen to start the game on the right wing away at Sheffield Wednesday. It started in the car park at Elland Road. I got on the coach and sat at a table of four opposite Gary Speed and David Batty, who was by the window. I can't remember who was next to me, but I do remember that I was sat in Carlton Palmer's place. He gets on and says, "Snowy, that's my seat." You have to remember that the YTS boys used to travel with the first team away from home, but we'd be making the teas and coffees, getting the sandwiches and just catering for the senior players. We would sit on a big bed at the back where six of us would congregate, all squashed in. Anyway, Carlton is not about to let this go: "Snowy, that's my seat."

'I said, "No, I'm sat down, mate, and that's it."

'Then Gary Speed begins winding him up: "Carlton, he's not getting out of your seat."

'I stood my ground. I'd already had a few spats with Speedo on the training ground, mainly me holding my own, because you had to do that to survive. Now he's pressing Carlton's buttons. In the end Carlton tries to grab me, and I can see the steam coming off the top off his head. Now the two of us are rolling around on the backseat having a scrap, fighting over this one spot. Carlton isn't even playing in the match. He is on the bench. I refuse to back down. In the end it is done and dusted. I sit down in the seat and he sits somewhere else.

'I felt comfortable there because I was cleaning Gary Speed and David Batty's boots at the time. Professionally, Carlton should have allowed me to have the spot because I was in familiar territory with two players I spent a lot of time with. I was still YTS at the time, not even a pro, but you have to have that determination. It was a tough learning curve breaking into the first team, and it was a period where I felt I had to show my strength in every way. I'm there in the first team, I've worked hard to get there, and I'm not about to be pushed out of a chair by someone who is not playing. That's what it's all about. When you are playing you can do this, when you are playing you can do that. And I was playing and he wasn't. 'I can't remember too many of the other YTS lads falling out with the pros like I did. That's where I got my nickname "Snowy" from: because I settled well, and I didn't care. I used to be in the ground early, and one day I remember seeing all my kit – shirts and shorts – covered with the word "Snowy". Batts and Speedo had got a marker pen and scrawled it over everything. It was part of being accepted. Arguments helped that. I settled well because I'd had that spat with Carlton and I had another with Speedo after an argument over an offside decision. I said, "Speedo, watch your offsides." He went mental, so I said, "Whatever, pretty boy." And he went mental again.

'You had to be tough, but that's how the name came about. It beat "Dog Shit Boy". Whenever I speak to the old pros now, like Gordon Strachan, Macca or Chris Whyte, the name they use is Snowy. It was never Noel, not even with the gaffer and the coach Mick Hennigan.

'On the way to the ground for my debut I was nervous, excited and apprehensive. I was thinking about my game and picturing certain things that were going to happen before the match started. I was getting my brain into gear. It was a proud moment, for sure, because it was everything I'd been building up for. I thought about all the training sessions and all the running I'd done with my dad. It was all for this moment, to have a place in the first team. And I'd done it ahead of time because I was still a YTS.

'I was always quietly confident it would happen, as I never felt I was far away, especially with Leeds not having too much to play for coming towards the end of the season. Knowing how well I did that year, I knew I had everything the manager was looking for in terms of height and speed. I could hold the ball, I could head, I could finish and I could bring others into play. I was a little bit different to someone like Jamie Forrester. I think I was a little bit more made for the Leeds United team.

'I found out I was playing, because in the corridor by the changing rooms there was always a list of players. I was in the

starting eleven with the subs listed below and I was, like, "Wow!
OK." It was kind of like one of those moments where you
take a step back and your heart feels like it is going to come
out of your chest. I was thinking, "This is unbelievable. I'm
really going to put this shirt on for the first time." It was an
immense feeling. Nerves and apprehension merged, and I was
just hoping I'd do everything right and everything well. You're
always going to make mistakes, because it's a different level
you're playing at against seasoned professionals. But, god, it was
some feeling, and we would have won the game if John Lukic
hadn't dropped a corner in the last minute, with David Hirst
popping it in to make it 1-1. Lee Chapman had scored for us.
'I was happy with my performance. Plenty of touches and I
remember one of my crosses being headed just over. After
the first ten minutes I settled down, but it was a bit surreal
playing alongside the guys I had only been training with. The
crowd were brilliant too. There's always pressure on any player,
but when you are a Leeds lad and a Leeds fan you put more
pressure on yourself. You want to do well for everyone, not
just the family but the other fans as well, and the manager
who'd put faith in me and had always been there to help. And
of course the players, as I didn't want to let anyone down.
That's how it was in that era. Training was the same as we
played. If there was a tackle there to win you'd go through it.
'On the right wing I had energy and pace. I could get
involved from there attacking wise and I had the height
as well – corners against, corners for, things like that. As
debuts go it was a special night, and I felt it went pretty
well. We were that close to getting the win, which would
have been nice away from home in a Yorkshire derby
'It was May by then and there was only one game left, with
Carl Shutt coming back in. The following season is when it
kind of all started for me. At the start of that season my shirt

number went from a high one to a low number. I knew then that I was part of the manager's plans. I was aggressive and he liked the way I played. Good energy, stamina, I was pretty much the whole package you want from a centre-forward. I was confident too. I knew I wouldn't be starting every game because I was young, but reckoned it'd be the majority of them. The gaffer trusted me and I knew I wasn't far off. Even if I started on the bench I knew I'd be getting on, and it proved to be like that – bits and pieces. I knew there were signings coming in and I had to keep up. Names were being bandied about and new faces were being brought into the dressing room, but competition is healthy, and it felt that way back then.

'Striker-wise I was up against Lee Chapman, Brian Deane, Phil Masinga and Rod Wallace. I knew I could play with all of them. I had more athleticism than Brian Deane and was a bit quicker, but he was a bigger man and had a lot more strength than I did, and he was more dangerous aerially. Even though I was 6 foot 2 inches I felt my game was on the floor, which it proved to be for most of my career. I didn't score many goals with my head. Me and Brian were different kinds of players but similar in many aspects. The gaffer also had the option of pairing Brian with Phil Masinga, who was more like me – athletic, good at running in and around the channels, linking up play. Rod Wallace could play out wide or through the middle like me. I could play left or right wing and drop into that midfield role as well as up front. I'd been tested and people knew I could play those roles. It was no different when I went to Coventry and played four different positions in one game at Liverpool, including right-back. Gordon Strachan was the Coventry manager then and he knew from my time at Leeds that I could adapt and play anywhere. I was actually top scorer for Coventry, with 13 goals from the left wing.

'In my first season at Leeds Nigel Worthington, Chris Whyte,

Chris Fairclough and Gary Kelly were all there. And, as I mentioned, Phil Masinga. There was one incident, between Phil and Lucas Radebe, who came together, and Tony Yeboah – the African players used to love a bit of Versace. When I say Versace, I'm talking massively naughty patterned shirts, which were right in your face and worn with plain jeans. We'd always be saying to them, "What are you wearing?" All those gold emblems and multi-colours going everywhere. I always remember one afternoon doing a double session with Phil at Fullerton. At the side of the banqueting suite on the back of the West Stand were some metal stairs going up to a flag-pole. I was not involved in this bit [of the session] so I grabbed Phil's Versace shirt while they were working on finishing and I went up the steps and hooked it onto the flag. I pulled out a lighter and waved it around as I shouted, "Phil, Phil."

"Don't you do that, Snowy. No, no, no!" 'I wasn't actually going to do it, but maybe there was a gust of wind and the lighter caught the silk, or something, but it just went up in flames. I could see Phil edging nearer the gate to the car park and I flew down the metal stairs as fast as I could. He started chasing after me, and I tell you, I could not have chosen anyone worse to try to outrun. Phil just didn't run out of steam. And he was steaming all right. I felt like I was running for my life and I'd got that jelly-leg on. I was thinking, "Oh my god." In the end I had to cut off down one of the side streets. He was still in his boots and his training kit as he searched for me down the streets. We had a few wry smiles afterwards, but even though he said it was a good joke, he still had the look that said, "I want to kill you." It was that sort of friendship. He got a bit over-aggressive in training after, but nothing too much, as I told him I'd just buy him another rubbish shirt. I did, and it was for a stupid amount too. 'We did have a great camaraderie in that team. We were very close, the lot of us. I think being a young lad and being introduced into that environment because I knew Speedo and Batts proved a massive help. We were all integrated because the youth team was always brought in to do the set-pieces and play against the first team so they could exploit certain roles. It would be like, "This is what Liverpool do and how they set up." So we would set up like Liverpool and then work on set-pieces to see how we could hurt them and test out new things. We would be kind of pawns on the training ground for the first team to practise against. It meant we were always playing with each other and that camaraderie and feistiness was there, as we didn't just allow them to walk over us. You had to be aggressive and train as you play. That's what we did back then and it was the same with the youth team.

'I worked my two-year YTS to get my professional contract. I think there were only two or three of us who won the FA Youth Cup in 1993 who were kept on. It shows you how difficult it was to make the next step and get a contract.

'The step-up to the first team and the Premier League was big. There's no name on the teamsheet that you don't recognise. You look at it and you see names like Ljungberg, Vieira, Petit, Henry, Roy Keane, all these names. At Liverpool you had Ian Rush, with Robbie Fowler coming through, and remember Eric Cantona was around after having left Leeds for Man United. It was a gulf, a different feeling, a bigger challenge.

'Elland Road always stood out for me when it came to stadiums, but I used to love going to Anfield too, with all the history behind it. "You'll Never Walk Alone" used to ring out and they used to play with different balls then. We'd play with the Premier League balls which were Mitre, but they had the Adidas Tangos. So a week before playing Liverpool we had to practise with the Adidas Tangos. They were a lot lighter and used to fly off your feet. I used to love going there, through the gates and down the stairs, and then seeing that famous crest as you came out onto the pitch, which was always immaculate. It was a good ground for me. Tottenham's White Hart Lane was another, as was Highbury.

'I scored my first Premier League goal against Arsenal in August 1994. It was at home and it was a night match. I was on the bench and it was a tight game. Ian Wright had gone close a couple of times for them. It was the second half at a packed Elland Road and I'd been warming up constantly. Then Howard Wilkinson called me over and said, "Snowy, get stripped, you're coming on." Quick word with the fourth official and the assistant Mick Hennigan put his arm around me and said, "This is your job – go out and get me a goal."

'As soon as he said that I thought to myself, "I'm going to just shoot from anywhere. Just have a go, Noel, just have a go." So I had that in the back of my mind. I'd had lots of chances the season before when keepers had made saves they never should have done, and but for them I would have had my first Premier League goal for Leeds ages ago. But I hadn't. I felt the pressure. I needed to score. It had been a very long wait. It was Gary McAllister who flicked it on and I had no idea whereabouts I was on the pitch, I really didn't. I was kind of lost in the moment. Then the voice in my head was saying, "Shoot from anywhere, Noel. Shoot from anywhere."

'So the ball's come. I'm under pressure from Tony Adams, who is behind me, and the ball has kind of kicked up off the turf and I've turned with my chest and, without even looking, I know Tony has gone. With that turn, the ball is bouncing nicely and I think, "I've done this so many times in the rugby-ground car park, outside my mum and dad's house, against the railings, hitting half-volleys, day in and day out." It is sitting there nicely and I think, "I need to cut across this." It dips right in front of David Seaman, the England number one. I think it's a mile out. I am watching it for what seems a long time. I see it kind of moving because I've cut across it on the half-volley and Seaman dives to his right-hand side. Just at the last minute the ball makes a little turn and I know he's completely lost the flight. It's bounced in front of him and it's gone over and into the back of the net.

'I just stood there. Then every Leeds player jumped on my back. I think the last one to pile on was Gary Kelly, from when I've watched it back afterwards. It was just one of those moments. What a feeling! All the chances I'd had were leading up to that moment, and none of the ones I'd hit sweetly enough had gone in. This is probably the one that shouldn't have gone in but did. These things happen, and I suppose it was the kick that I needed to get the monkey off my back. When I look back it just gives me shivers. It was at the Kop end as well, and the crowd went mental, absolutely mental. The only way I can describe it – it was like I used to be when I was on the Kop watching. I'd be jumping up and down on people's backs, going crazy, back when it was all-standing. It was just immense. Probably like winning the Super Bowl with the state you grew up in. The feeling and the tingle that I had with everyone piling on knowing it was the winning goal, because it was 89 minutes, or something. Everyone knew that was it. We'd won the game. How we'd won the game we just didn't know. How the hell the ball had gone in we didn't know either. But it had, and no one even cared. It was very early in the season and it was one of those moments we needed as a team, and I needed as a striker. It kind of gave us that lift and a bit more confidence.

'Making your debut, winning the FA Youth Cup and scoring your first Premier League goal all in the space of a season were all highlights for me at Leeds. Add to that winning the European under-18 championships with England in 1993. I went on to play under-21's for England and I was tipped to and should have made my senior England call-up when I was at

Coventry, but I wasn't chosen by Glenn Hoddle. Maybe I could have gone with the Republic of Ireland to a couple of World Cups but Paul Hart pushed me towards England. He said, "You want the Three Lions on your chest and your heart." He took me to Lilleshall for my first game. I said to my dad, "Whoever comes in first, I'll play for them." It would have been nice to get my first senior England cap, and a lot of people think I should have done at the time, but I wasn't at a fashionable club at Coventry. However, if I'd played for Ireland I would not have won the European under-18s championship with England. I chose a harder route to get any kind of caps. We won the Euros at Nottingham Forest's City Ground, beating Turkey 1-0. I came on and nearly scored. The tournament was great because there were a lot of top players there and it was a good era for England. Even David Beckham couldn't make it into the under-18s. We had Paul Scholes and Gary Neville, and I roomed with Sol Campbell throughout the tournament. He was a really good laugh, and we've stayed in touch. It's always nice to see him. 'I think what gave me a little bit of edge is that I came from a working-class background. When you are raised on a council estate in Burmantofts you naturally get an edge. Times were different back then and we had to work hard for everything. I had a milk round at five in the morning, followed by a paper round. I'd earn my money and do whatever it took. I think we were a bit tougher because we had to do certain things to get by. With my dad being disabled from the waist down I had to do things that any 11-year-old shouldn't have to. I had to look after him. All these things toughen you up.

'As I mentioned, I didn't have much of childhood as my dad would later take me to the gym and running in the hills. So when I signed professional forms I made up for it. Was I bad? No worse than most, but maybe more than some. I was lively, put it that way. I had the gold card as a regular for Mr Craig's nightclub. A lot of things came off the back of playing for Leeds: boot deals, full-page spreads in *Shoot!* magazine, girls, everyone tipping you for a long career at the club because you are the rising star.

'All of it means the pressure mounts. There's more attention with every game you do well in. You have to figure out how to deal with that, and with someone being more aggressive to you. How? You'd give him a kick first and get into his head. There was a lot more talking back then and a lot more grappling, gripping your skin, a lot more dirty tackles; a lot more trying to get into your mind by saying things. Some people would sink, but I'd be like, "You're having a bit back, here."

'Arsenal were the worst for it. The entire back four were always at it: "I'm going to break your fucking leg. You do that again and I'll break your nose, you little c**t." I remember playing at Highbury and we were just doing the warm-up when Ian Wright broke away and walked up to the halfway line shouting at David Wetherall, "Wethers, I'm going to twist your fucking spleen inside out in this game."

'To be fair, he did – and he did that to many defenders. It was all about psychological warfare, getting into people's heads, nipping them, twisting the skin, grabbing them at corners, trying to get that reaction out of them. Wisey [Dennis Wise] was brilliant at it. He'd grab hold of your thighs at corners and wait for you to lash out and get you sent off, whilst he's like, "See ya later." All these little dirty tricks of the trade showed it was a lot more aggressive back then. The defenders were tougher, physical characters. Adams, Keown, Bould and Dixon, with Winterburn, at Arsenal were all renowned for it. They were a team that had everything. Similarly, Man United were a different side without Roy Keane. Without a shadow of a doubt, if he wasn't on the teamsheet we had a chance of beating them. If he was playing, maybe not.

'I had a good experience against them at Elland Road. It was a live Sky game on a Sunday and the noise at Elland Road was deafening. Eric Cantona was back at Leeds, but for the old enemy, and I was starting. I just had a strange feeling about that day, even when I woke up. The sun was shining when I looked outside and it made me feel happy inside. I was ready for this. I'd had a few more games by then and I felt more confident and stronger. Plus, you don't need any more incentive when it's Man United. The fans want it, we want it, and everyone was up for the scrap. No motivational talks were needed for this game. And everything kind of went for us, although I dislocated my finger twice during the game. The first time was just before David Wetherall scored at the Kop end in the first half and someone came in and tackled me. The top of my finger was pointing at a horrible right angle. That meant I'd run across to the sideline with it looking like I was giving them the finger. The physio got hold of it and I looked at the sky while he pulled it and put it back in again. While all that was going on Wethers scored the first goal.

'The game was competitive and going well. Andrei Kanchelskis was lively on the right but Nigel Worthington was dealing with him. Gary Kelly on the opposite side was up against Ryan Giggs, but we were matching them and actually beating them at playing football on our patch. First half, I was getting the ball and laying it off. They weren't getting close to me. I was linking up well and had nearly scored from a corner. I set up Brian Deane for a great chance but he fluffed his lines. Any other day he'd put it in the back of the net. We had a rhythm to our play and we all felt good. In the second half I was on the left-hand side. Nigel Worthington played it down the line to me and then I tried to find Rod Wallace. It came back off a player and then Kanchelskis came to tackle me. I was standing sideways on the touchline, pretty much, and I handed him off. Then I'd three more to deal with. I think it was David May and Gary Pallister, or Steve Bruce, but I can't remember – and Denis Irwin. I just thought, "Right, I'm just going through the lot of you here." I was positive and used my pace plus a bit of trickery to get into the 18-yard box. I was kind of stretching a little bit, looking to clip it to the far post, but I couldn't get it there. Luckily, Brian Deane showed intelligence from a striker, because we are always told to make sure you get across the front post. I'd just managed to hook it across to the six-yard box where Deano had made a run from far to near. The keeper Peter Schmeichel had gone down but Deano managed to put it over the top of him. Goal! The feeling then was probably as good as scoring. People ran to me just because I set it up. People ran to Deano too, but I created it out of nothing. I was getting better and better each week, feeling more confident, and I knew what I could actually do with the football and my own ability. I thought it was going to last for ever.

'I certainly didn't think it was going to end so quickly. I was 20, and Gordon Strachan had already gone to Coventry with Big Ron Atkinson. Tomas Brolin had come in off the back of the World Cup; Tony Yeboah too. I don't know why they bought Brolin, but it meant that I was free to leave. Also they couldn't pay for the East Stand. Older players wouldn't leave, and they had had offers in from Coventry on the back of Gordon going there. In the end they'd had two or three offers for me and, after having said no to them, they eventually had to accept one. That was my Leeds career cut short when I wasn't even in my prime. I had so much more to offer and so much more to give. Coventry got it from me, but maybe if I'd been at Leeds I would have played for England. Instead, I became Coventry's main signing and striker alongside Dion Dublin.

'I didn't know it was coming at all. I knew nothing about the rejected bids. It was on a Sunday morning and I'd been out. Strangely enough, my agent had come down and he'd been in my spare bedroom in Horsforth. We'd been out with a couple of the lads from the team and I knew they were having a Christmas do on that Sunday at Elland Road. So I got a phone call really early, when my head was throbbing. The voice on the other end sounded familiar, but I wasn't sure.

"Snowy, it's the gaffer."

"Fuck off. Who is it?"

'Again I hear, "Snowy, it's the gaffer here."

'As soon as he said that he didn't have to say anything more. So Howard Wilkinson is suddenly asking me to come to the stadium as he needs to see me. I just literally lay there in bed crying. I knew what it meant. I went into the spare bedroom and saw my agent and said that the manager had rung me and wanted me to go and see him. He said the same as I was thinking: "You're leaving."

'I went down and saw Carlton Palmer with his wife and children at the Christmas do. Then I went downstairs and had a chat with Howard. He said they'd accepted an offer. I was upset. I was crying again. I hate reliving those moments now. In my eyes I'd only just started, because I knew what player I could become. I'm a Leeds lad and I know what it's all about. It's my club. Not in a million years did I think I'd be leaving, not that soon anyway. If I did I thought it would be at least another three, maybe four years, but even then I didn't believe it possible. Howard told me I had to go to Coventry that day where me, Gordon and Big Ron would discuss personal terms at a hotel. 'It was a bleak Christmas. I walked out of the West Stand reception at Elland Road bawling my eyes out. Outside Billy Bremner was there.

"What's up?"

"I've been sold."

'He smiled, just gave me the biggest hug, and said, "You'll be back."

'He was right. I played for another ten clubs, but the truth is: we are Leeds – and I never really left.

For more details on Tales from Elland Road
books and events please visit
www.talesfrom.com